Certified
Six Sigma
Green Belt
Exam

SECRETS

Study Guide
Your Key to Exam Success

**CSSGB Test Review for the
Six Sigma Green Belt
Certification Exam**

Dear Future Exam Success Story:

Congratulations on your purchase of our study guide. Our goal in writing our study guide was to cover the content on the test, as well as provide insight into typical test taking mistakes and how to overcome them.

Standardized tests are a key component of being successful, which only increases the importance of doing well in the high-pressure high-stakes environment of test day. How well you do on this test will have a significant impact on your future, and we have the research and practical advice to help you execute on test day.

The product you're reading now is designed to exploit weaknesses in the test itself, and help you avoid the most common errors test takers frequently make.

How to use this study guide

We don't want to waste your time. Our study guide is fast-paced and fluff-free. We suggest going through it a number of times, as repetition is an important part of learning new information and concepts.

First, read through the study guide completely to get a feel for the content and organization. Read the general success strategies first, and then proceed to the content sections. Each tip has been carefully selected for its effectiveness.

Second, read through the study guide again, and take notes in the margins and highlight those sections where you may have a particular weakness.

Finally, bring the manual with you on test day and study it before the exam begins.

Your success is our success

We would be delighted to hear about your success. Send us an email and tell us your story. Thanks for your business and we wish you continued success.

Sincerely,

Mometrix Test Preparation Team

Need more help? Check out our flashcards at:
http://MometrixFlashcards.com/SixSigma

TABLE OF CONTENTS

Top 20 Test Taking Tips

1. Carefully follow all the test registration procedures
2. Know the test directions, duration, topics, question types, how many questions
3. Setup a flexible study schedule at least 3-4 weeks before test day
4. Study during the time of day you are most alert, relaxed, and stress free
5. Maximize your learning style; visual learner use visual study aids, auditory learner use auditory study aids
6. Focus on your weakest knowledge base
7. Find a study partner to review with and help clarify questions
8. Practice, practice, practice
9. Get a good night's sleep; don't try to cram the night before the test
10. Eat a well balanced meal
11. Know the exact physical location of the testing site; drive the route to the site prior to test day
12. Bring a set of ear plugs; the testing center could be noisy
13. Wear comfortable, loose fitting, layered clothing to the testing center; prepare for it to be either cold or hot during the test
14. Bring at least 2 current forms of ID to the testing center
15. Arrive to the test early; be prepared to wait and be patient
16. Eliminate the obviously wrong answer choices, then guess the first remaining choice
17. Pace yourself; don't rush, but keep working and move on if you get stuck
18. Maintain a positive attitude even if the test is going poorly
19. Keep your first answer unless you are positive it is wrong
20. Check your work, don't make a careless mistake

Overview: Six Sigma and the Organization

Contributions of Philip B. Crosby and George D. Edwards to quality control

Philip B. Crosby is perhaps best known as the author of *Quality is Free*, one of the seminal texts of quality control. This book was extremely popular with American managers. It extolled the benefits of doing things right the first time. Crosby also is known for promoting his four cardinal rules of quality management: the performance standard should be set as zero defects; quality is the same thing as conformance to requirements; quality is achieved by preventing defects; and the measure of quality's value is the cost of nonconformance. George D. Edwards is known as the first president of the American Society for Quality. He was the head of the inspection engineering department for Bell Telephone Laboratories. He was instrumental in advancing their groundbreaking quality assurance program.

Contributions of W. Edwards Deming to quality control

W. Edwards Deming is known as one of the fathers of quality control. One of Deming's primary insights was his use of statistical methods to promote quality control. He also championed the distinction between common- and special-cause variation. His most widely known contributions to the field are the so-called "seven deadly diseases of the workplace" and "14 points for management." According to Deming, seven "deadly diseases" can afflict organizations. These "deadly diseases" include: a lack of consistency in planning; emphasis on short-term profits; poor performance evaluation systems; excess turnover among employees; overreliance on the metrics that are the easiest to obtain; excessive medical costs; and excessive liability costs, typically associated with legal departments. Deming argued that all of these problems can drain resources, personnel, and ultimately profits from a business, and they are even more insidious because often they go noticed.

14 points for management
Maintaining consistent purposes and adopting a new philosophy: W. Edwards Deming outlined fourteen points for management. These points are basic guidelines for the promotion of quality. The first point is that managers should maintain consistent purposes. These purposes should be to maintain high product or service standards, to be competitive in the marketplace, and to keep people employed. Deming was reacting to what he perceived as pervasive short-term thinking in the business world. He advocated the establishment of research and development programs enable constant innovation and progress within the organization. Deming's second point is that businesses must embrace whole-heartedly the new quality philosophy, including lobbying governments for laws that foster quality. Deming believed that the entire organization, from senior executives to new employees, had to believe in the merits of quality improvement programs. This point was in part fueled by

nationalist sentiment during a period in which American businesses felt threatened by foreigners, particularly the Japanese.

Eliminating dependence on inspection and ceasing to award business based on price alone:
Deming's third point for management asserts that inspection should be eliminated as much as possible. In Deming's view, inspection programs are ineffective because they spot mistakes only after they occur. He believed that setting up programs to stop mistakes before they happen is far better. In addition, inspection programs can be costly to establish and maintain. Deming said that businesses should spend this money on improving production processes. The fourth of Deming's points for management is that business should not be awarded solely because of price. Instead, businesses should create a measure of total cost and use this measure to make their buying decisions. As much as possible, businesses should have a single supplier for each part, product, or service, because this practice will enable them to monitor quality and establish beneficial relationships. Deming approved of long-term relationships with suppliers because these relationships create greater opportunities for customization and optimization. Also, he asserted that businesses would be better off in the long run if they purchased top-quality goods rather than goods that cost the least.

Constant quality improvement and on-the-job training: Deming's fifth point for management is that production and service systems should be improved continuously so costs can be decreased continuously. Constant quality improvement can be achieved only by unceasing attention to the desires of customers. Businesses always should be improving the methods by which they gather and use customer information. Customer desires change over time, so data collection never should cease. Deming distinguished continuous quality improvement from solving problems, which is an ineffective way to achieve constant improvement over the long run. Deming's sixth point for management is that all employees should receive on-the-job training. Employees should receive training in all areas that pertain to their work, and managers always should understand the tasks of their subordinates. Effective training requires steady and productive communication between all layers of the organization. Also, training programs should be based on concrete and specific performance standards.

Establishing leadership and eliminating fear: The seventh of Deming's fourteen points for management is to establish effective leaders. The purpose of management should be to set a proper example rather than to monitor the behavior and performance of subordinates. If training is effective and standards are clear, employees should not need constant supervision. Managers always should do their jobs with an eye toward improving quality. In addition, managers should have the authority to resolve issues they observe in the workplace. The eighth of Deming's points for management is that fear should be eliminated as a source of motivation. Deming observed that many organizations terrorized their employees with the constant threat of demotion or firing. He felt that this was an ineffective way to inspire loyalty and quality. Moreover, employees should feel comfortable enough in their jobs to consider possible innovations or to raise questions with their superiors. Likewise, managers should not be afraid of receiving comments or complaints from their subordinates.

Reducing interdepartmental barriers and reducing pressure on the workforce: The ninth of Deming's fourteen points for management is the reduction of barriers between departments. Deming promoted interdepartmental communication as a method for reducing waste and improving quality in all areas. To some extent, employees need to be trained in all other departments. In complex organizations, of course, this practice is not always possible; nonetheless, at the very least managers should be familiar with the tasks and responsibilities of the other departments. Deming observed that many businesses segmented their departments and evaluated performance as such, so departments in a failing business might appear to be thriving. To Deming, this seemed like an ineffective system. He was in favor of linking all departments together. The tenth of Deming's fourteen points for management is that workers should not be pressured with short-term production goals. Instead, workers should be encouraged to embrace a holistic, long-term program for quality improvement. Constant exhortations and work targets, in Deming's view, contribute to anxiety and lower production among workers. Goals never should be set for individual employees, but instead for larger groups.

Eliminating quotas and ineffective management styles: Deming's eleventh point for management is split into two parts. The first part is a declaration that production quotas should be eliminated. In many factories, managers establish concrete production goals. For Deming, this sort of leadership is ineffective because continuous improvement always will affect the appropriateness of targets. According to Deming, encouraging employee pride and promoting quality is more sensible and will generate better results than mere focus on quotas. In a more general sense, the second part of this point for management is managers' responsibility to avoid basing their decisions on short-term objectives. Deming believed establishing a positive long-term plan and adhering to this plan made more sense than pursuing immediate gratification in the form of quotas or sales targets. By emphasizing continuous quality improvement, managers create the conditions for success.

Promoting employee pride and emphasizing quality over production: The twelfth of Deming's fourteen points for management is divided into two parts. The first part is the promotion of employee pride. Deming felt that employees will do a better job when they are given the chance to feel responsible for their work. Furthermore, he felt that businesses should look for opportunities to link employees with their work, such as giving employees control over over multiple tasks in production or service provision. Deming felt that fear and anxiety in the workplace were obstacles to employee pride and therefore to quality. Employees always should be taught to emphasize quality over numerical production. Indeed, the second part of the twelfth point for management is the promotion of quality over production. To Deming, this practice meant the abolition of merit systems, which reward success within the business rather than improvement of the business. Deming believed that rewarding employees for the volume rather than the quality of their work set up bad incentives. In other words, this improper emphasis would encourage employees to make decisions that harm quality.

Encouraging self-improvement and universal buy-in: Deming's thirteenth point for management is the creation of self-improvement programs. Deming believed that organizations thrive when employees feel that their personal goals align with the goals of the organization. One way to achieve this alignment is by helping employees better themselves through in-house education opportunities. Employees always should believe that effort and self-improvement can lead to promotion within the organization. The last of Deming's fourteen points for management is universal buy-in. Deming believed all members of an organization should subscribe to the new vision of quality improvement. Managers are responsible for informing and encouraging their subordinates. All the employees will not be able to adhere to the quality management program unless it is made plain that adherence will advance their own as well as the organization's interests. Moreover, Deming felt that managers always should be alert for opportunities to increase employee participation in quality improvement.

Contributions of Armand V. Feigenbaum to quality control

Armand V. Feigenbaum was an aggressive promoter of total quality management. He outlined four key actions businesses needed to take in order to implement TQM programs: establishing standards; measuring conformance to these standards; resolving issues hindering conformance; and continuously planning for improvement. Feigenbaum was also known for his Nine M's of quality: markets, management, men, money, motivation, materials, machines, modern information sources, and mounting product requirements. By *mounting*, Feigenbaum mean consistently improving. Feigenbaum was one of the first quality specialists to insist that quality standards be assessed from the perspective of the customer rather than the perspective of the business. He argued that all standards should pertain to qualities for which a customer would be willing to pay. In the past, businesses frequently ignored customer desires.

Contributions of Joseph M. Juran to quality control

Joseph M. Juran emphasized the idea that quality control always should be considered from the perspective of the customer. Juran advocated deep involvement by management in the process of quality improvement. His version of quality management had three main components. First, he advocated quality control and the use of statistical control methods for the mitigation of problems. He also promoted quality improvement and the use of the breakthrough sequence for resolving persistent problems. Finally, Juran promoted quality planning, and in particular annual quality reviews for the purpose of enshrining quality control efforts. Walter A. Shewhart, meanwhile, combined economics, engineering, and statistics in his work. He is widely known as a top engineer at Western Electric and Bell Telephone Laboratories and as the author of *Economic Control of Quality of Manufactured Product*.

Contributions of Kaoru Ishikawa and Genichi Taguchi to quality control

Kaoru Ishikawa was one of the main promoters of total quality control in Japan, where the field would become wildly popular and even more sophisticated than it had been in the United States. Besides the diagram named for him, Ishikawa is credited with developing the quality circle, in which work groups rather than lone employees resolved problems. One of his most popular ideas was that employees should be involved as much as possible in quality management issues. Genichi Taguchi was another top advocate of quality management in Japan. He wrote *Design of Experiments*, which included the first signal-to-noise measurement. Taguchi was employed by Japan's Ministry of Public Health and Welfare, where he promoted the use of statistics in quality management.

Six Sigma

Six Sigma is a program for improving business processes. The name is derived from the Greek letter sigma, or σ, used in statistics to indicate the standard deviation for a particular set of data. The standard deviation suggests the amount of variation between the members of the data set. Statisticians describe variation in terms of units of standard deviation, or sigma units, in order to provide a more accurate picture. Imagine a process that can be represented graphically as a bell curve. The centerline of the process is a time of 25 minutes, meaning that this is the average time required to complete the process. If the standard deviation is 30 seconds, then six standard deviations, or 6σ, would be either 22 minutes or 28 minutes. The general intention of Six Sigma is to improve all business processes such that six standard deviations will fit between the mean and both the upper and lower acceptable limits.

Process cycle efficiency metric

The measurement of process cycle efficiency is used to determine the most useful and positive ways to improve cycle time. The process cycle efficiency metric is used most often during the analyze stage of DMAIC. The general method for calculating process cycle efficiency is to divide value-added time by process lead time. Process lead time is calculated by dividing the number of items in a process by the number of times the process is completed in an hour. This calculation is known as Little's law. A process can attain a maximum process cycle efficiency of 100% if all the activities in the process add value. However, it is more typical for processes to approach 25% efficiency after the implementation of lean strategies. The reasonable value for efficiency depends in large part on the type of activity. Creative activities usually have efficiency values of approximately 5%, although lean management strategies have been known to increase this figure up to almost 25%. Transactional activities, on the other hand, sometimes can reach efficiency values of up to 50%.

Lean

Lean is a comprehensive system for decreasing waste and increasing cycle times and quality. The tools of lean (e.g. 5S, velocity, spaghetti diagrams, level loading, and process cycle efficiency), are used in every phase of DMAIC. Many of the ideas of lean date back to Henry Ford, but the credit for assembling and updating the system goes to Taiichi Ohno, an employee of Toyota in the 1970s. In Japan, the philosophy is called *muda*. The general strategy of lean is to identify activities that add value and activities that do not add value. As much as possible, lean businesses try to eliminate activities that do not add value. These judgments always are made from the perspective of the consumer. Lean methodology is very similar in this respect to Six Sigma.

Transparency, velocity, and value
The lean philosophy emphasizes three areas: transparency, velocity, and value. Transparency is easy access to useful information. A business has achieved transparency when processes can be observed and measured. Errors should be noticed immediately and rectified. Velocity, meanwhile, is the speed with which processes are completed. The ultimate measure of velocity is the interval between a customer's order and the delivery of the good or service. In lean methodology, velocity is sometimes called flow. The goal of lean is to reduce process lead times and enable the business to respond quickly and agilely to customer requests. Finally, value is the set of qualities or characteristics for which a customer is willing to pay. The goal of lean is to increase value and diminish waste. Value always is assessed from the perspective of the customer.

Inventory
In lean methodology, inventory and work-in-progress are considered drags on progress rather than assets. A lean business will try to keep very little inventory on hand and instead will strive to respond quickly to customer orders without relying on the storage of works-in-progress. A general habit involves finishing work in progress before handling new orders, which slows down production. Lean emphasizes other strategies for improving velocity. For instance, business can find ways to increase the number of completions per hour or eliminate redundant or unnecessary process steps. A business could improve velocity by decreasing errors or waiting time. A business also could improve velocity by decreasing the necessity of moving resources or personnel. When velocity is increased through these strategies, value tends to increase as well.

Kaizen philosophy

Kaizen is a Japanese philosophy that governs all aspects of business. In kaizen, constant efforts should improve the quality of the business. These improvements

- 7 -

are continuous and subtle, unlike those produced by Western-style innovation. In kaizen, improvements are small and frequent. Many improvements are based on the insights and experiences of lower-level employees, in contrast to the Western business model, in which changes typically result from executive orders. The initial concern of the kaizen business is attracting and maintaining good employees. The kaizen philosophy asserts that good employees will make good processes inevitable. Kaizen can be successful only with adequate training, defined operating practices, and buy-in from all employees. Furthermore, in kaizen, constant communication exists between employees at all levels. Kaizen is one of the more effective systems of total quality management.

Flow, pull, and perfection

In the kaizen philosophy, flow is the quality of continuous process accomplishment. The goal of kaizen is to create continuous flow through the organization rather than improving limited areas of a process. When a process has good flow, materials and information do not wait between activities. Businesses tend to create inefficiencies when they focus only on flow in one or two areas. Instead, flow should be considered from the perspective of the entire business. Pull is another concept in kaizen. In this system, pull means that each activity in a process should receive only the necessary materials and resources when subsequent activities are demanding the process be completed. In other words, instead of pushing resources through the process chain, it is more effective to have them be drawn along by the vacancies created by completed projects down the line. Finally, in kaizen the term perfection is defined as the ultimate goal of continuous improvement. By eliminating waste and streamlining processes, an organization can approach perfection.

Error-proofing strategies

Error-proofing, often referred to with the Japanese term *poka-yoke*, is a system for preventing defects in production processes. The poka-yoke philosophy asserts that preventing errors is better than detecting them, so processes should be analyzed rigorously and improved so mistakes occur less often. One form of error-proofing is auto-correction systems, which reflexively adjust to changing external conditions. Another form of error-proofing is an automatic shutdown, which stops a machine or process if conditions for an error exist. A final form of error-proofing is the warning signal, which of course depends on the presence of a human operator. Nevertheless, a warning signal can be an effective alert that an error is about to occur. Error-proofing strategies can be expensive to implement and may slow processes at first, but in the long run these strategies will save money and time that would have been wasted on mistakes.

Value stream mapping

Value stream mapping is a communication tool for Six Sigma professionals. It depicts the flow of materials and information through an organization. Most value stream maps have two versions: a current state and a future state. The future state map depicts the process after planned improvements have been made. Ideally, the future state version of the value stream map will be less complicated than the current state. Value stream maps are effective when they identify waste and redundancy in processes. Each activity in a process should be represented with a shape on the map. Furthermore, each activity should be accompanied by the following information: cycle time, down time, in-process inventory, path of information, and path of materials. After a current state value map has been produced, it should be examined for steps that do not add value. These steps should be eliminated or minimized.

Value stream analysis

The value stream is the entire series of activities that create value in a product or service. The addition value is considered from the perspective of the customer rather than from the perspective of employees or management within the company. During process mapping, the Six Sigma team will divide the activities into three categories: value-added activities, business-value-added activities, and non-value-added activities. Value-added activities, as the name suggests, create value for the customer. Business-value-added (BVA) activities do not create value for the customer, but are necessary anyway. These activities sometimes are referred to as Type 1 waste. Some examples of BVA activities are marketing, design, and delivery. Non-value-added (NVA) activities create value for neither the customer nor the business. The goal of Six Sigma projects is to eliminate as many NVA activities as possible.

Theory of constraints

The theory of constraints is an approach to improving processes by focusing on their most problematic areas. These problem areas are known as constraints. Even the smoothest processes will have some areas of constraint. Improvement efforts will be devoted to improving performance in this level without sacrificing quality elsewhere. Essentially, the theory of constraints encourages businesses to improve continuously by diagnosing weaknesses and addressing them. There is no end to work under the theory of constraints: once one area has been improved, another becomes the constraint and must be addressed. In order for work to be successful, the business must be able to develop effective strategies for maximizing the potential of the constrained area. This action of maximizing the potential is known as exploiting the constraint.

DMADV and DMAIC

DMADV and DMAIC are both Six Sigma methodologies, but they have different applications. DMADV stands for define, measure, analyze, design, and verify, while DMAIC stands for define, measure, analyze, improve, and control. DMADV is the appropriate methodology for new products and processes because it includes a design phase. Another instance in which the DMADV methodology might be useful is when DMAIC has proven ineffective at bringing an existing process up to sufficient quality standards. If a process needs to be created from scratch or subjected to a comprehensive overhaul, DMADV is appropriate. DMAIC, on the other hand, is suited for gradual improvements of existing processes and products. DMAIC is appropriate for bringing processes and products into alignment with customer requirements and quality standards.

IDOV

IDOV is one of the common methodologies of Six Sigma. It stands for identification, design, optimization, and validation. In the identification phase, the business determines the needs of customers. Also, the business will create an effective business model and establish a Six Sigma team. In the design phase, the team uses critical-to-quality metrics to determine the best methods for processes. In the optimizing phase, the Six Sigma adjusts the factors that contribute to processes until the best outputs are achieved. Finally, in the validation phase, the Six Sigma team makes any necessary changes to the new process. IDOV is the methodology most commonly associated with design for Six Sigma, or DFSS. Unlike DMAIC, DFSS emphasizes defect prevention rather than reduction. Also, DFSS is more concerned with the creation of new, high-quality processes than with the incremental improvement of old processes.

Define

Objectives of the define stage

The method for problem solving in Six Sigma is expressed as the acronym DMAIC, which stands for define, measure, analyze, improve, and control. The first state, define, focuses on identifying and articulating a project's important characteristics, including identification of the goals, objectives, and scope of the project. The Six Sigma team also should make explicit the team members and sponsors, as well as the proposed schedule for the project. The Six Sigma team should define the desired result of the project, otherwise known as the deliverable. In considering the process to be improved, the team should identify the stakeholders, the input/output structure, and the functions involved. The other component of the define stage is selecting and assembling a team able to accomplish all of the proposed goals. The members of this team must be able to work together well and must all have a solid understanding of the task before them. Moreover, all the members of the team should agree with the desirability of successfully completing the project.

Process definition

The first major step in the measure stage is to create a comprehensive process level map of processes as currently performed. In other words, during this stage the group defines and clearly describes all of the activities they aim to improve. This is a much more detailed and comprehensive version of the top-level process map created in the define stage. A detailed process map typically requires the participation of expert employees. This participation is important especially because employees may have a vastly different conception of process sequence than their superiors. Often, employees will have streamlined or modified a process without notifying management. Judging the beneficiality of customizations made by employees is unnecessary and potentially harmful. The primary concern at this point is to create an accurate map of the process as currently performed.

Top-level process definition

The most common tool for top-level process definition is the flowchart. A flowchart does a good job of representing process sequences graphically, with a minimum of verbal description. The look of a flowchart is very easy to read. When the team wants to identify inputs, outputs, and stakeholders, SIPOC (suppliers, inputs, processes, outputs, customers) analysis is more appropriate. Another tool is the process map, which is similar to the flowchart, although it contains more detail. A process map indicates who is responsible for each activity in the process. A comprehensive Six Sigma project might include more than one of these tools for top-level process definition. The primary aim of these representations is to inform stakeholders and other people peripheral to the project. A top-level process definition will not contain enough information to explain each process in depth.

Obtaining customer information

Areas businesses tend to ignore

Many businesses pride themselves on their aggressive outreach to customers but fail to gather information about non-customers. Businesses should be concerned with the characteristics of people who choose not to buy their products, so they can consider how to appeal to these people. Businesses also should develop ways to identify customers who switch to a competitor but do not make a complaint or give any other alert of their defection. Sometimes, customers will switch to a competitor not because they dislike any aspect of their original purchase but because the competitor makes a special offer. A business should identify product features that cause customers to defect. Businesses also should develop ways to obtain information about customers who become dissatisfied with a product after its warranty period is over. These customers often see no point in contacting the manufacturer, who then loses a valuable source of information about customer desires and product failures.

Comment cards and formal surveys

Many businesses rely on comment cards and formal surveys for information about how customers view the business' products and/or services. The most basic metric obtained in these ways is customer satisfaction, and more specifically, how customer satisfaction is affected by various characteristics. Comment cards are left in places where customers will be, and customers voluntarily complete them. For this reason, very satisfied and very dissatisfied customers are overrepresented, because they are more likely to be motivated enough to fill out a card. A formal survey will attempt to gather information from a more representative sample of customers, although these surveys are often returned by the same highly motivated customers. Surveys are more effective when they ask customers for specific information about their preferences.

Focus groups

A focus group answers questions about the services or products of a business. The members of a focus group may be customers or non-customers. They may be a random group of citizens or members of a target demographic. Sometimes, businesses assemble focus groups of people from demographics in which they do particularly well or particularly poorly, in the hopes of learning the secrets of their success or failure. The typical format of a focus group is for the attendees to be presented with a sample of the product and then asked to give their impressions. The focus group will be more valuable when more specific and targeted information is obtained. In most cases, the members of a focus group will be compensated, but the leaders should make it clear that participants are to be honest. Focus groups provide direct insight into customer perceptions, but they are more expensive than other methods of obtaining customer information.

- 12 -

<u>Field intelligence</u>

Field intelligence is the information obtained by employees through their normal interactions with customers. For instance, a salesperson will gain insights into the desires of customers without ever asking a direct question. Any employee who talks or works with customers will pick up valuable information. The key for a business is to establish and maintain channels for this information. Open lines of communication must exist so field intelligence can reach the higher levels of the organization. Some businesses establish mechanisms for gathering extra field intelligence. For instance, a retail store might set up video cameras in order to facilitate study of customer behavior. The store might be able to identify those areas where customers are more likely to linger.

<u>Customer service and complaint management</u>

Many businesses obtain most of their information about customers from routine customer service and complaint management. Executives in Six Sigma businesses commonly meet with customers personally. Some businesses establish programs in which every employee spends a certain amount of time dealing with customers. This practice prevents employees from pursuing goals that are distant from the concerns of the customer. Six Sigma businesses pay special attention to customer complaints. Any reports of error or malfunction are assessed and organized so pervasive problems can be noted. A good company makes it easy for customers to complainand for these complaints to be heard. Complaints are an excellent source of ideas for new Six Sigma projects.

QFD

Quality function deployment, typically called by the initials QFD, is a system for ensuring that customer requirements are aligned with product and process requirements. Quality function deployment most often is used in the analyze and improve stages of DMAIC. In these stages, QFD is used to plot strategies for fulfilling customer requirements. The basic process of quality function deployment is to establish customer requirements, known as whats, and design requirements, known as hows. The customer requirements are what needs to be achieved, and the design requirements are how they will be achieved. A number of tables are used to assess the importance and significance of various design requirements in the promotion of customer requirements. If a customer requirement, or what, has very few or no design requirements, or hows, then improving the process may be possible. When there are hows without whats, the process may contain some non-value-added activities that can be eliminated.

Scorecards in performance measurement

Scorecards are a common tool for measuring performance. They break performance down into a series of categories, each of which is assigned a few top-level metrics. The most typical version, known as the balanced scorecard, contains four categories: financial, customer, internal, and innovation. The customer metrics should be based on satisfaction, while the internal metrics should relate to those aspects of company performance most closely aligned with quality. The innovation dimension, sometimes called "learning and growth," should feature metrics of how much the business is working to stay current and improve its processes, products, and services. The balanced scorecard gives a quick, comprehensive look at the organization's performance. Some critics, however, charge that the balanced is an overly simplistic view and does little to suggest possible areas for improvement.

Project charter

A project charter is an overview of the project. It changes as the project moves along, so team members and sponsors will remain on the same page. Management should approve the project charter in order to give the project legitimacy and informed guidance. A good project charter will establish clear deliverables, so its success or failure can be measured. Also, a good project charter will direct employee efforts to the right areas because it will identify the key variables that affect performance at all levels. A project charter will ensure that a proposed project does not interfere with other work performed in the company, because it will make public the intentions of the team. The project charter also will ensure that Six Sigma efforts are directed to the most important aspects of performance, and that they deal with processes integral to the business in the future.

Project statement, scope, and deliverables
The project charter is a document in which the most important details about the project are codified. Of course, this document will be subject to revision as necessary. One of the hallmarks of the DMAIC structure, and indeed of Six Sigma itself, is a willingness to rethink first principles at any time. The first step in composing an effective project charter is to make the problem statement explicit. The team should ask itself why the project is necessary. The reasons clearly should be integral to the optimal function of the business. Indeed, a project charter should express deliverable in terms of actual output and in a manner approved by the financial department of the organization. In most cases, it is necessary to confirm the reasonableness of the estimate with the finance department before writing it into the charter. The charter also should include a reasonable estimation of the project scope, based on the data collected thus far.

Schedule, stakeholders, and team composition
A project charter must include a provisional schedule. This schedule should include specific dates on which established objectives and goals are to be met. Although the schedule established at the beginning of a project is unlikely to survive the imposition of unforeseen events, project leaders should be as specific and prudent as possible. The project charter also should include a complete identification of the stakeholders in a project. Stakeholders are those persons who influence a project or are affected by a project. Along with an identification of the stakeholders, a project

charter should include a list of the team members. Of course, the list of stakeholders and team members will feature significant overlap.

Finalizing a project charter

A project charter should include an appointment for an initial meeting, at which the team members will discuss and consent to the scope, deliverables, and provisional schedule to be included in the charter. This meeting allows team members to become acquainted with one another if they are not already and to voice any initial concerns or ideas related to the project. Having agreed upon the core items of the project, the team should map the top level of the process to be improved. This information should be entered into a new, updated version of the charter, which then should be submitted to the sponsor for approval. Obtaining this approval is important so both project participants and sponsors understand the nature of the work about to be undertaken. This way, any initial misgivings can be addressed without much loss of resources.

Problem statement

A project charter typically will begin with a problem statement in which the author defines an adverse situation in the business, or the target of the proposed project. If possible, a problem statement should provide measurable evidence of the problem's existence. It also should describe the problem in terms of poor outputs. The collection of objective data related to the problem may not be easy, particularly if the problem relates to a new business process or a process previously not addressed. However, the project charter should include as much preliminary data as possible, with the understanding that it will be updated as the project moves along and more data becomes available. The measure stage of the DMAIC model is an opportunity for the team to refine its charter through direct acquisition of data. The presence of objective data is important because it justifies the decision to direct resources toward the project.

Defining the business need

A project charter needs to identify the specific business need or needs that will be addressed by the proposed project. In other words, the charter must name the business processes that will be improved by the successful completion of the project. As with the problem statement, this section of the charter should include as much objective data as possible. It may be difficult for the author to estimate the value of the project to specific business processes, particularly if this estimate is based on minimal and preliminary data in the problem statement. However, if possible the charter should refer to specific metrics such as the number of defects, schedule, or profit. Many Six Sigma theorists recommend that all projects have a clear and measurable benefit to the customer. Comprehensive project charters will address business needs related to the customer, stakeholders, and other employees.

Statement of objective and identification of resources

A complete project charter should include a statement of objective in which the author provides a definition for the intended result of the project. Most Six Sigma experts recommend expressing this result in financial terms, since such terms are easy to understand and unlikely to vary. Other measures, like defects per million or return on investment, may be used but are more subject to variation and unforeseen influences. A complete project charter also will identify the resources required for the project. The efforts and time of the team members are not included in this summary. The resources may include equipment, materials, computer time, databases, and other employees. The resources required by a project are not only those resources necessary to improve the process, but also those necessary to collect and analyze data along the way.

Project scope

A project charter will include a clear description of the project scope, or the particular part of the problem to be targeted. For a number of reasons, it is better for projects to have a limited scope. Otherwise, objectives can become team members can become disgruntled, and resources can be wasted when a project stretches out indefinitely. In general, Six Sigma projects should take no more than four months. Longer projects run the risk of losing key members. If the members of a team have a vision that cannot be realized within four months, they should consider whether the grand project might be divided into multiple smaller projects. Indeed, the composition of the charter is an excellent time to consider the appropriate scale for team efforts. Often, a team will decide to solve a particular problem, only to discover that it depends on a collection of smaller problems that must be resolved first. In such a case, the team may want to conduct a series of smaller projects rather than grouping the entire problem in one project.

Sponsors

A project charter must identify the project's sponsors, or the managers who will provide guidance. The sponsors will provide funding to the project, give the team members access to resources, and inform other managers about the project's existence and intentions. One of the sponsor's jobs is to create enthusiasm and support for the project, so the project will receive any possible assistance from other employeesAs a result, the charter should identify appropriate sponsors. The sponsors should be selected from the departments most relevant to the project. In cases where the project participants are drawn from a number of different departments, the sponsors may need to be drawn from the ranks of those managers who oversee multiple departments. Such selection will make it possible for the project team to receive all the required support. Also, team members should avoid selecting sponsors who are already involved in several other projects.

Stakeholders and team members

A project charter should identify the stakeholders as clearly as possible. Stakeholders are all of the people and groups affected by the problem being addressed and potentially affected by the project as it progresses. In Six Sigma, the team should use a top-level process map to identify all of the affected groups. Affected groups may include customers, suppliers, other employees, and specific departments within the organization. The charter also should identify the members of the project team, or all the stakeholders participating in the project. Most projects are headed up by a single black belt, with one or more green belts representing each relevant department. Some projects may require the participation of experts or skilled employees. In rare cases, a Six Sigma project team will include a facilitator to ensure that all members of the team work together effectively.

Deliverables

A project charter should include a clear and measurable identification of the deliverables created by the project. A deliverable is any fungible benefit or advantage. Identifying deliverables is important because it enables the overall success or failure of the project to be assessed. Establishing targets for deliverables allows the project to be judged on its own terms. One common mistake is to list aspects of the project's method as deliverables. For instance, some project charters will identify the data obtained during the project as a deliverable. This is misguided, in part because the data would not be necessary if not for the existence of the project. Although systems such as statistical process control have utility for an organization beyond the scope of the project in which they are created, they should not be counted as deliverables. If possible, deliverables should be placed in financial terms.

Schedule

A project charter should include some form of schedule, even if the schedule likely will be modified once the project begins. The schedule should include the date on which the charter was approved by the sponsor as well as the start and completion dates. A good charter will indicate the dates on which each phase of the DMAIC schedule will be complete. This process is known as a phase-gate review. The authors of the charter will use critical path or program evaluation and review technique (PERT) analysis to set the target dates. The schedule typically is expressed as a Gantt chart, in which each phase of the project is defined, and the prerequisites and required resources are listed. Each of the phases of the DMAIC schedule should be subdivided into a set of activities.

Work breakdown structures

A work breakdown structure is a diagram that depicts the parts of a problem or process. These diagrams are useful when a problem seems overwhelming, because they break the problem down into manageable "sub-problems." Work breakdown structures are most useful during the define and analyze stages of DMAIC. In the define stage, work breakdown structures are combined with Pareto analysis to organize problems before solutions are applied. A work breakdown structure also may be useful at this time to eliminate less important areas of a project and thereby ensure adherence to a schedule. In the analyze stage, work breakdown structures are used to organize all of the issues and complaints to be handled during the improve stage. The completion of a work breakdown structure often suggests that different solutions should be applied to different parts of a general problem.

<u>Creation and interpretation</u>
A work breakdown structure is created first by breaking a problem into components. Each component of the problem subsequently should be broken down into categories. These categories should represent the different ways the particular problem can occur. The intention of the work breakdown structure is to reduce complex problems to a collection of discrete and manageable issues. The organization of a complex situation creates a map for problem solving that can be used by members of different departments. A comprehensive and effective work breakdown structure will create material for other data-organization charts such as Pareto charts. The information displayed on a work breakdown structure would be prioritized on the resulting Pareto chart.

Pareto charts

A Pareto chart is a form of bar graph in which problems are ranked according to their urgency. Each of the categories represented along the horizontal axis of a Pareto chart are exclusive, meaning that no single issue can fit into multiple categories. This characteristic is important because the category distinctions on a Pareto chart are largely subjective. Pareto charts are used during the define and analyze stages of DMAIC to guide the dispersal of resources and time to the most important issues. The categories on a Pareto chart are organized in descending order from left to right, according to whatever metric is deemed most appropriate. Most experts recommend that the metric be related either to count or to cost. Percentages and rates are not valid metrics for a Pareto chart.

<u>Creating a Pareto chart</u>
The first step in creating a Pareto chart involves identifying the correct categories. These categories should be non-overlapping and fungible. The count/cost metric will be along the left axis of the chart, and the identities of the categories will be along the bottom axis. Data should be collected over the same interval for each category. The categories will be placed in descending order from left to right. An indication of the percent demarcations, or the percent of total cost/count represented by each variable, will run along the right vertical axis. The cumulative percentages from each bar are indicated with a line ascending from left to right. This cumulative aspect of the Pareto chart makes percentages and rates unacceptable as data. In order for the chart to work, the data must be additive.

<u>Interpretation</u>
Pareto charts attempt to isolate the categories that contribute the most to count or cost. In addition, the cumulative line aspect of the chart indicates the degree to which resolving problems with the most pressing issues would improve performance. The traditional method for using a Pareto chart involves identifying the left-most categories that approximate 80% of the count or cost. These categories are the most important areas. A Pareto chart with a steep cumulative line is better because in such a chart, the value is concentrated in the left-most categories. A relatively flat cumulative bar is less helpful, because this arrangement indicates no

problems as more important than the rest. When a Pareto chart is flat, the categories have been subdivided too much. In such instances, regrouping into a few large categories may bring about a better result.

Process metrics

Process metrics must be reliable, repeatable, and reproducible. Otherwise, they cannot be considered effective illustrations of process characteristics. At the same time, measurements must be specific and detailed enough to distinguish between the effects of process alterations and process noise. As much as possible, metrics should relate to actual targets of business strategy and should result from cooperation between employees. Before any metrics are applied, employees from several different departments should judge them. If possible, metrics should be related to actual services provided to customers. Finally, metrics should pertain to values critical to quality, schedule, or cost, as these factors are the three most important variables in any process.

Identification of process metrics

One of the key tasks of the measure stage is to identify process metrics. Typically, quite a few process metrics can provide useful information about a particular process. These metrics tend to relate to schedule, cost, or quality. Factors critical to schedule (CTS) have a direct bearing on the completion date of the process. Factors critical to quality (CTQ) have a direct effect on the desired characteristics of the product or service. Factors critical to cost (CTC) have an impact on materials, labor, delivery, overhead, inventory, and/or the cost to the consumer of the good or service. As much as possible, these metrics should be customer-focused and transparent: that is, they should provide immediate objective data that can be analyzed. Moreover, these metrics need to be obtained with measurement systems that are repeatable and reproducible.

Critical-to-schedule metrics

Cycle time is the most common critical-to-schedule metric. Cycle time is the duration required for the completion of a defined process. It may be called delivery time, order processing time, or downtime. The improvement of critical-to-schedule issues begins with making the distinction between process steps that add value and process steps that do not add value. Six Sigma professionals often use process efficiency and velocity numbers to assess value added relative to cycle time. In most Six Sigma projects, cycle time is considered secondary to metrics related to quality or cost. A project that focuses exclusively on reducing cycle time is more likely to compromise quality. However, it can be useful to baseline quality and cost metrics and then work to reduce cycle time. This ensures that quality will not be affected by any time-saving adjustments.

Critical-to-cost metrics

Critical-to-cost metrics identify areas of a process that significantly raise the expense. Critical-to-cost metrics should include not only the typical cost of a task, but also the increased cost of errors in the performance of this task. The likelihood of an error should be included in the metric. For instance, the metric should consider how long it will take to redo or repair a product made incorrectly. If a lag time exists in a process, the critical-to-cost metrics should include the cost of keeping materials on hand. The effects of errors on cost tend to multiply as the product moves farther down the path. In other words, a mistake made in the design phase will be significantly less expensive to resolve than an error in the manufacturing phase. The amount of money required to align a product or service with quality baselines is known as the cost of quality.

Critical-to-quality metrics

One of the more common critical-to-quality metrics is yield, or the amount of completed product divided by the amount of product that began the process. Obviously, a business would like to have yield equal 1 (or 100%). The difference between perfection and reality is known as the scrap rate. If a process had a yield of 95%, the scrap rate would be 5%. Yield is a useful metric, although it does not indicate where in the process errors occurred. Also, yield does not distinguish those pieces of scrap that can still be salvaged. A slightly more advanced metric is throughput yield, or the average percentage of units with no defects. When multiple steps in a process are considered, Six Sigma teams use rolled throughput yield, which measures the expected quality level after several steps.

Gantt charts

Gantt charts are used to identify the critical path of each dependent task in a particular project. The critical path includes everything that has to be done to maintain the project's timing. Any process not on the critical path may be slightly delayed without extending the overall duration of the project. These activities are said to have built-in slack time. At the beginning of a Six Sigma project, distinguishing the tasks that are on the critical path is important. The use of Gantt charts typically is restricted to the define stage of DMAIC. The intention of this chart is to identify those tasks that, if truncated, would lead to an overall cycle time reduction. In addition, a comprehensive Gantt chart will make it possible to place all project activities on the schedule. In some cases, a Gantt chart may be used during the improve stage to confirm the reduction of critical path cycle time.

Creation
Gantt charts are useful for identifying the critical path of a process. The first step in the creation of a Gantt chart is to make a list of all the tasks that have to be completed in the project. After these tasks have been placed in the order in which they need to be performed, it should be determined whether some tasks may be

performed simultaneously or whether some tasks require the completion of previous steps before they may be initiated. On a Gantt chart, jobs that can be done at the same time are placed on parallel paths, and other jobs are placed in sequence. Within each parallel path, there may be serial tasks. However, if one of the parallel paths can be completed more quickly than another, then some slack time can be built in to that path.

<u>Interpretation of Gantt charts</u>
Gantt charts help businesses create the fastest-possible schedule for a process. The most important benefit of a Gantt chart is that it indicates areas within the process that can tolerate lag. Essentially, a process that is not on the critical path may be initiated a little late or finished a little early. For every task, though, there will be some time by which it must be initiated and some time by which it must be finished. Of course, it is not always possible to obtain a precise measure for the duration of a particular task. For this task, it may be necessary to perform program evaluation and review techniques (PERT) analysis. PERT analysis can gauge the probability of a task being completed within a certain amount of time.

PERT analysis

Program evaluation and review techniques (PERT) analysis is used to estimate the time required by various processes. Furthermore, PERT is an essential part of scheduling and cycle time analysis in which hard data on the duration of certain process steps may be unobtainable. PERT analysis uses probability techniques to determine a best guess about durations. PERT analysis is used during the define, analyze, and improve stages of DMAIC. In the define stage, PERT analysis is used to identify the steps in a process with the most influence on the overall duration of the process. In the analyze stage, PERT analysis is used to determine the critical path of a process cycle. During the improve stage, PERT analysis is used to confirm improvements in the cycle time.

<u>Process</u>
The first step in program evaluation and review techniques (PERT) analysis is to isolate activities on the critical path. This isolation can be done with any number of charts, such as an activity network diagram. For the purposes of PERT analysis, it should be assumed that activity times follow a β distribution. The estimated duration of each activity therefore is calculated with the formula $\mu = (a + 4m + b)/6$, in which a is an optimistic estimate of the time, b is a pessimistic estimate of the time, and m is the most likely time. The calculation for estimated standard deviation for each activity is calculated with $\sigma = b - a/6$. The central limit theorem suggests that the total time for all tasks should be in a normal distribution. Adding up the times for the tasks on the critical path yields a measure of total time. The upper predicted limit for total time is equal to the total time + 1.96 × standard deviation. The lower predicted limit for total time is equal to the total time – 1.96 × standard deviation. These are good estimates for the best and worst possible durations.

- 21 -

Project status report

Project status reports begin with a current schedule and brief description of the project. A project status report should include a list of the action items, or the tasks to be completed by assigned team members at particular times. The project status report also will include lists of roadblocks, or hindrances to progress not yet resolvable by specific actions. A project status report also will include a list of the data obtained during each phase of the project. Finally, the project status report should list any items that should have been finished but have not yet. These are called outstanding items. Project status reports typically are issued once or twice a week and every time one of the DMAIC phases is completed. Copies of the report are sent to the sponsor, team members, and any other relevant stakeholders.

Affinity diagrams

Affinity diagrams organize a collection of issues, problems, or ideas so they may be utilized effectively. The diagram is so called because it identifies the affinities, or similarities, between seemingly disparate ideas or problems. Organizations using affinity diagrams often discover unforeseen relationships between variables. These diagrams often are used at the beginning of a process, when the team is trying to gain a primary understanding of the problem. An affinity diagram can be useful for building a consensus when members of a team have divergent interests and knowledge bases. However, affinity diagrams may be used in every phase of the DMAIC process. One common result of an affinity diagram is the identification and elimination of redundancies in thinking.

Creation
To create an affinity diagram, teams begin by identifying the target issue or problem. The next step is to have each member of the team list a few issues that impact this target. It is important to collect as many ideas as possible. Once the ideas are collected into a general list, they can be organized into categories. Redundant items may be discarded. Discussion or even argument about the logic of sorting is typical. The team leader should administer this part of the process calmly and proactively. Once the categories have been labeled and filled, the group should come up with header cards for each title. The titles may be useful for nominal group technique or in the creation of a prioritization matrix. If the process is a success, then the main ideas listed on the header cards will indicate the most important drivers to be addressed for the achievement of objectives and goals. It should be noted that affinity diagrams do not require objective information; instead, these diagrams are tools for organizing the subjective impressions of team members.

Prioritization matrix

A prioritization matrix ranks choices. This tool is used primarily to build consensus in a group setting. Six Sigma teams typically use one of two methods for creating a

- 22 -

prioritization matrix: either the full analytical method or the consensus-criteria method. Prioritization matrices primarily are used during the define and improve stages of DMAIC. In the define stage, prioritization matrices are used to help groups pick the projects most important to the organizational objectives and goals. A prioritization matrix can be an effective tool for comparing customer desires with process also metrics. As much as possible, a business wants to measure the qualities of a process or product important to clients. In the improve stage, a prioritization matrix can be used to confirm the alignment of projects with customer requirements.

Full analytical method of creation

The full analytical method of creating a prioritization matrix begins by listing options and the criteria required to evaluate those options. It Phrasing the criteria as targets such as lower cost or greater employee satisfaction is important In the full analytical method, the first matrix contains comparisons of every criterion with every other criterion. Six Sigma teams typically use a numerical rating system in which 10 indicates the most importance, 1 the average level of importance, and 1/10 the least importance. In the second matrix, each option then is evaluated with respect to each criterion. Each option receives a final score compiled of his or scores on the weighted criteria. Most statistical software programs provide a summary matrix in which all of the options are ranked.

Consensus-criteria method of creation

When there are too many criteria or options or too little time to create a prioritization matrix according to the full analytical method, the consensus-criteria method can be a useful alternative. In this method, the initial matrix is discarded, and the team simply distributes a hundred points across the criteria in accordance with perceived importance. This method is slightly more subjective in its assessment of importance, but it is far less time-consuming. After the criteria have been weighted, they are compared with the options. The final score for each option is calculated by multiplying its score for each criterion by that criterion's weight. The larger the product, the more important the option. Both the full analytical and consensus-criteria methods of creating a prioritization matrix make an essentially subjective exercise into something a bit more structured.

Matrix diagrams

Matrix diagrams indicate the relationships between several items in multiple groups. A matrix diagram is a table in which the value in each cell indicates the strength of the relationship. Matrix diagrams often are used during the define and improve stages of DMAIC. In the define stage, these diagrams are used to pick projects that will contribute to the achievement of organizational objectives and goals. Also, matrix diagrams can be used in the define and improve stages to examine the similarity between customer desires and process metrics. The first step in the creation of a matrix diagram is to identify the items for comparison. Six Sigma teams often transfer the categories from some other chart, such as an affinity diagram. The next step is to use consensus decision-making rules to evaluate the relationships between each pair of values. In this subjective process, the team should perform carefully and according to an organized protocol.

A few different types of matrix diagrams exist, each of which may be useful in particular circumstances. In a directional system, arrows suggest the nature of the relationship between each pair of items. Sophisticated directional systems have weighted arrows that indicate the direction of causation as well as the importance. In a numerical matrix diagram, numbers perform the same functions as weighted arrows. For example, on a ten-point scale a 5 might indicate a moderate relationship in one direction, while a 1/5 indicates a moderate relationship in the opposite direction. In a plus-minus system, a plus sign indicates a relationship and a minus sign indicates the absence of a relationship. In a symbol system, finally, triangles, circles, and squares indicate characteristics of each relationship. Matrix diagrams typically have final rows and columns that tally up the total importance of each item or process. The team then can identify the items and processes that have the most significance.

Process decision program charts

Process decision program charts (PDPCs) break a process down into its component tasks, with special emphasis on potential problems and solutions. As such, these charts are a useful tool for brainstorming protocols for handling crises that emerge during processes. Process decision program charts are used during the analyze and improve stages of DMAIC. In the analyze stage, they are effective for identifying the underlying causes of recurrent problems. In the improve stage, they may be effective at linking possible problems with probable solutions, so contingency plans can reinforce process. The top of the chart will name the process, and below this top line the chart will list the steps required to complete the task. These steps are presented in order from right to left. Below each step, one or two sub-steps may be necessary. However, it is recommended that the chart be kept simple. Under each step or sub-step, the chart should list some potential problems. Provisional solutions should accompany each of these possible problems.

Prediction of benefits

The Six Sigma team must justify their proposed solutions by predicting the benefits to be obtained. First, the team may need to use a prioritization matrix to show how proposed solutions are aligned with the most pressing needs of the business. A common metric for proposed solutions is earnings before interest and taxes (EBIT), although this metric requires fixed and variable cost figures. EBIT is calculated by multiplying volume by the difference between price per unit and variable cost per unit and then subtracting fixed cost. When a proposed solution has varying benefits over time, these benefits can be evaluated with net present value analysis. Furthermore, some teams calculate the internal rate of return if the net present value is invested. These sophisticated methods allow the team to determine the probabilities of achieving various levels of savings or profit.

Evaluation of process failure modes

The initial goal during the improve stage of DMAIC is to optimize the process flow. Once this optimization is complete, the team will evaluate the new failure modes. In other words, the team will now examine the new operating conditions or process flows for possible sources of deviation. Once these conditions or flows are identified, the team will brainstorm possible solutions. These problems and potential solutions often are depicted on a process decision program chart, which looks a bit like a tree diagram. The process decision program chart is a good first step, but it usually must be supplemented by failure modes and effects analysis, or FMEA. A comprehensive FMEA concludes with the generation of a risk priority number (RPN), indicating the influence of a particular failure on overall performance. The team then must develop mitigation or elimination strategies for the most significant potential failures.

Team formation

Successful Six Sigma teams usually do not cooperate without conflict at the beginning. Indeed, most groups must pass through some conflict and reconciliation periods before they can work effectively. The trajectory of a team has been codified according to four stages: forming, storming, norming, and performing. In the forming stage, the members of the team are getting to know one another, and so for the most part they are on their best behavior. At this point, the team has not yet begun working seriously enough to inspire much conflict. In the second stage, storming, the team begins its work in earnest, and differences between the members begin to emerge. During this stage team members will begin to assume different roles. The team leader must exercise control during this stage so conflicts can be resolved beneficially. In the norming stage, the team members settle their differences and settle on compromises that make effective work possible. This stage is called "norming" because team members are agreeing to normative behavior for the group. In the performing stage, the team operates at an optimal level because members have learned to work together.

Team leader

A team leader is responsible for establishing and maintaining protocol, the set of rules by which the team will operate. The team leader also is charged with continuously realigning the team's efforts with the original goals and objectives. A team often will need to review first principles in order to stay on track. A team leader also is responsible for handling any conflicts that should arise during the project. A team leader will be responsible for planning and administrating the team's meetings. The team leader must meet with stakeholders and project sponsors in order to keep them apprised of the group's progress. A team leader must work continuously to improve the team's performance, first by helping members brainstorm and then by refining solutions through the use of data analysis.

Common problems and solutions for teams

Team dynamics can be rough, especially during the early stages of a Six Sigma project. In order for a team to thrive, the roles must be defined and appropriate. In some cases, roles will be assigned by the team leader. At other times, it will be better for team members to settle into roles as they become familiar with one another. This latter process usually entails some conflict at first. A team also will struggle if members are not held accountable for their actions. Accountability is the responsibility of the team leader. Teams should meet only when necessary but should stay in regular communication throughout a project. When meetings do occur, they often are hijacked by members who digress, go off on tangents, or rudely reject the ideas of others. This behavior should be stopped immediately by the team leader. A similar group problem is groupthink, in which the members of a team are reluctant to disagree or do not have enough experience to come up with alternate solutions. Groupthink can result from having too little expertise in a team.

Effective change agents and issues that diminish buy-in from stakeholders

Most people claim to embrace change, but few people actually do so. Employees typically are reluctant to give up their old habits. To be effective change agents, the members of a Six Sigma team must first acknowledge the importance of having all employees on board with changes. Change agents take conscious steps to increase buy-in, commitment, and participation. Buy-in may be lacking if the goals of the project are unclear. Employees are more likely to participate and conform when they see how the proposed solutions will benefit them personally. However, employees will be skeptical if they believe the project team has prejudices and preconceived solutions. If the project team does not communicate regularly with the employees, the employees will lose faith in the project. Finally, buy-in will be reduced if the project's goals are too diffuse. Having a number of small projects with single targets is better than one giant project with several targets.

Responses to conflict

Avoidance
Five basic responses to conflict exist. These responses include avoidance, accommodation, competition, collaboration, and compromise. Avoidance is the least cooperative and assertive way to resolve a conflict. If a person notices a conflict but fails to bring it up or pursue it, he or she is avoiding the conflict. This may seem an ineffective behavior in the business world, but in some situations, avoidance is the correct response to conflict. If the conflict is insignificant or the outcome is assured, avoidance may be the best approach. In other words, if there is no chance of getting one's way, it may be better to avoid a conflict. Avoidance may also be the correct response if tempers are already hot over some other issue. It may be preferable to

avoid a conflict until the members of the team have settled down. Another time to avoid conflict is when the possible consequences of disagreement vastly outweigh the benefits of resolution. Finally, a team member may be justified in avoiding conflict if he or she feels other members of the team can do a better job of resolving the issue.

Accommodation

Accommodation is the suppression of one's own interests in order to serve the interests of another person may be served. Accommodation can be a valuable tool in conflict resolution, as long as it does not engender resentment. In some cases, it team members should accommodate one another. For instance, a team member always should accommodate if he or she recognizes personal error. Another time to accommodate is when the issue is clearly much more important to the other person. When an issue is trivial to one person in a disagreement, that person may be better off conceding the point and hoping for consideration in the future. Accommodation also is appropriate when the group is fragile and more conflict could be very damaging. Of course, excessive accommodation can inspire some members to dominate the team, and in some cases accommodation will lead the team to accept the incorrect solution.

Competition

One response to conflict is competition, wherein the conflicting parties do their best to win. As long as the competition is fair, it can be a great way to settle disputes and generate excellent work. Most people perform better when they feel they are up against a competitor. Competition can be as simple as civilized argument during a meeting. Using competition as a response to conflict is appropriate when some members of the team are undecided. A team member also should be ready to compete when an issue is vital to the success of the business. Competition is an appropriate response to conflicts that need a clear resolution. An objective form of competition settles a dispute for good. When competition is used to settle disputes, the team leader should ensure that team members are fair and nice to one another. Also, competition sometimes becomes a habit in a team, which can be detrimental to cooperation in the future.

Collaboration

Collaboration is the response to conflict wherein team members work together to find a solution. When two team members disagree, they may collaborate until they come up with a resolution they both support. Collaboration is an effective style of conflict resolution when both parties have good points. Collaboration also is appropriate when members of a team have different areas of expertise, and so it is a good idea to combine their perspectives. Collaboration works when the conflicting parties have some personal disharmony; the process of collaborating may help them work through these problems. Collaboration also is a good idea when cooperation will increase buy-in from other team members and stakeholders. One problem with collaboration is that it can take a long time. For this reason, it should not be used to

- 27 -

resolve unimportant conflicts. Also, collaboration can make room for too many viewpoints, which is a problem when some members of the team are inexpert.

<u>Compromise</u>
Compromise is a useful response to conflict when maintaining team harmony is more important than coming up with the best possible solution. Compromise, therefore, is not the right approach to ending crucial conflicts. It is appropriate, however, when two important members of the group are diametrically opposed on a key issue. If neither of these parties will give ground, a compromise may be the only way for the group to move forward. Compromise also can be the best course when no time exists for a lengthy debate or collaboration. Compromises can be very successful, but they sometimes leave the participants with lingering regrets. Also, compromises may produce mish-mash solutions that fail in the long run. Some problems require a clear, unified approach, and cannot be resolved through compromise. Finally, compromise should be avoided when it will disillusion some members of the team.

NGT

Nominal group technique (NGT) is a system for ranking non-objective data and is used primarily to create consensus or agreement in groups. Nominal group technique is used most commonly during the define and analyze stages of DMAIC. In the define stage, it is used to simplify project loads by combining redundant projects and eliminating unnecessary projects. In the analyze stage, nominal group technique helps teams agree on which solutions should be pursued. The first step in nominal group technique is to distribute paper to each team member. In the event of more than 35 options, each team member should receive eight pieces of paper; if there are 20 to 35 options, each member should receive six pieces of paper; and if there are less than 20 options, each member should receive four pieces of paper. Following discussion, each team member will select one option for each piece of paper he or she has received and indicate the option's rank on the paper. Then the papers are collected, and the weighted rankings are tabulated. The group then can focus on the most important and preferred options.

Measure

Basic objectives of the measure stage

During the measure stage of DMAIC, the Six Sigma team will focus on gathering the information necessary to complete the project. First, the team will attempt to define each relevant process in great detail. At the same time, it will be necessary to develop a group of metrics appropriate to the processes. No metric is complete until accompanied by a measurement analysis system that identifies and quantifies any common errors in the metric. In other words, the team will need to determine the ways in which the measurement system likely is inaccurate. The final general objective of the measure phase is to estimate process baselines. This objective enables the team to identify a reasonable starting point for the project.

Process maps

Process maps are clear, easy to understand depictions of the sequence of steps necessary to finish a process. One common use for process maps is to identify the amount and type of value added at each step in the process. Process maps may be used during all of the stages of DMAIC. In the define stage, they are used to record top-level processes. In the measure stage, they are used to record the lower process levels and reveal differences in the perceptions of shareholders. During the analyze stage, process maps are used to investigate the sources of variation or excessive cycle time. In particular, process maps are good at finding process complexities, shareholders, and inefficient locations. Process maps often are used during the control stage to tell shareholders about change proposals. During the control stage, process maps may be used to record process adjustments.

Creation and interpretation

On a process map, a symbol represents every step in a process. Although it is possible to use the entire set of ANSI symbols for flowcharts, it is more common simply to depict decisions with diamonds and other tasks with rectangles. All decisions should be framed as binary; that is, only two possible answers exist. In more sophisticated process maps, shading or shaping will indicate delays or measurement intervals. As with flowcharts, one of the clearest signs of inefficiency on a process map is a glut of decision points. The goal of process maps is to spot redundant, unnecessary decisions and tasks and to discover ways to simplify processes.

Identification of key decision points

Once the process map has been created, it can be used to identify the most important decisions made during the process. Team members will especially be alert to any areas that seem to require excessive decision-making, usually a sign of inefficiency. As much as possible, the team will want to reduce the number of decisions that have to be made every time a process is performed. All stakeholders must be aware that changes are not to be made to the process at this time. Since the process has not yet been measured, it is essential that all measurements reflect the process as typically performed. Otherwise, improvement efforts could be targeted incorrectly. The team leader needs to communicate this information to all stakeholders.

Flowcharts

A flowchart is a basic tool for recording all of the steps in a particular process. Flowcharts are used during the measure, analyze, improve, and control stages of DMAIC. In the measure stage, flowcharts can be used to map a process as it is currently being performed or to identify how different shareholders perceive a particular process or problem. In the analyze stage, a flowchart can be used to identify complications in a process that can lengthen cycle time or cause adverse variations. In the improve stage, flowcharts can be used to diagram possible improvements and changes. Finally, in the control stage, flowcharts can be used to map out processes that have been revised and improved.

Creation and interpretation
Flowcharts simplify communication by representing each task in a sequence with a symbol. Most organizations endorse the use of the symbols created by the American National Standards Institute. Some employees already will be familiar with the ANSI system, in which decisions are represented by diamonds and processes are represented by rectangles. Some flowcharts will incorporate different colors to suggest departmental divisions and time distinctions. Flowcharts are fairly easy to interpret, assuming the team already is familiar with the process. One thing to look for is a preponderance of decision points, as this occurrence may lead to unnecessary delays or adverse variations. The goal of process improvement is to reduce complications and unnecessary lags. Therefore, the interpretation of a flowchart always should be performed with an eye toward simplifying as much as possible.

Spaghetti diagrams

Spaghetti diagrams depict the movement of resources, materials, or personnel throughout an organization. Spaghetti diagrams are used during the analyze stage of DMAIC. These kinds of diagrams isolate wasteful movement, whether in regard to people or resources. The first step in the creation of a spaghetti diagram is to generate a map or floor plan of the relevant area. The site where the process begins is marked with a 1. The next destination for the person or material is marked with a 2, and a line is drawn between the 1 and 2. This process continues for the entire path of the person or material. Including landmarks and obstacles such as furniture and doors in the diagram is a good idea. Once the diagram is complete, it can be scoured for opportunities at simplification.

SIPOC

SIPOC (suppliers, inputs, processes, outputs, and customers) analysis provides a comprehensive look at a process. SIPOC is used during the define stage of DMAIC, when the Six Sigma team tries to identify each top-level process, as well as its stakeholders. In the context of SIPOC analysis, suppliers are those persons who contribute inputs to the process. Inputs are defined as all of the knowledge, resources, and information required to produce the desired output. A process is defined as any task that translates inputs into outputs. Accordingly, the outputs are the deliverables, or the products of the process. Finally, the customers are all of those parties that receive the deliverables (outputs). SIPOC is initiated with the creation of a flowchart or process map. Typically, the first category to be identified is the outputs. From there, locating the customers, inputs, and suppliers will be easier.

Cause-and-effect diagrams

Cause-and effect diagrams, sometimes known as fishbone or Ishikawa diagrams, are an easy and effective way to depict the reasons for a particular event. The typical layout of a cause-and-effect chart features the causes and effects listed in distinct boxes with arrows pointing from causes to effects. A cause *can* have more than one effect, and an effect *can* have more than one cause. Cause-and-effect diagrams are used during the analyze and improve stages of DMAIC. In the analyze stage, they are used to create innovative lists of possible process factors to be explored further in a designed experiment. In the improve stage, cause-and-effect diagrams are used to create lists of possible failure modes that must be considered when crafting a solution.

Creation and interpretation
The first step in creating a cause-and-effect diagram is making a provisional list of the possible relationships between the process and the outcome. Phrasing the target in terms of a problem is better than phrasing the problem in terms of a goal. All of the factors that influence a main problem will branch off from that main problem. For some problems, beginning with either the four Ps (people, plants, policy, and procedures) or the 5Ms and E (measurement, material, methods, machines, manpower, and environment) will be appropriate. Using these models can ensure that no significant influences are overlooked. The main causes should be connected to the problem, and subordinate clauses should be connected to the main causes. In especially detailed diagrams, several hierarchical levels of causes may exist. Cause-and-effect diagrams are primarily brainstorming tools, not final assessments, so it is important to include many different possible answers. Once all of the causes and effects have been outlined, the group should examine the diagram to see whether

certain categories exhibit a preponderance of causes. These categories may require further subdividing, or they may become targets for problem-solving efforts.

Process baseline estimation

Enumerative statistics

In process baseline estimation, enumerative statistics are useful for evaluating random samples from populations. For instance, these techniques can be used to determine whether two samples were drawn from a known population, as well as whether the samples were drawn from the same population. Enumerative statistics can determine whether samples represent the population, meaning that they were drawn without bias. Enumerative statistics can provide a confidence level, an assumed distribution, and a set of confidence intervals as well. In most cases, the confidence level will be 95%. Confidence intervals are the upper and lower boundaries for the value of the statistic given the data. The only problem with enumerative statistical methods is that they are drawn from a static, unchanging population. In Six Sigma, often it is necessary to obtain information about dynamic processes. For this, analytical statistics are required.

Analytical statistics

Analytical statistics can provide information about processes in action. These techniques distinguish common- and special-cause variation. Common-cause variation occurs consistently and always influences data in a similar fashion. Special-cause variation, on the other hand, is unpredictable in its occurrence and effects. Statistical process control charts create an operational definition of special-cause variation by noting the location and level of variation within a subgroup at each time in the process. If enough subgroups can be collected, the statistical process control chart will be able to predict the location and extent of special-cause variation. The key feature of analytical statistics is the consideration of time, which makes it possible to pinpoint the moments in a process that need improvement.

Central limit theorem

In some cases, there will not be enough (or good enough) data to establish a distribution. The central limit theorem is applied when the true distribution of a population is unknown. The central limit theorem, in short, asserts that the probability distribution of the sample means will approach a normal distribution as the number of samples increases, provided that they are simple random samples of uniform size. The central limit theorem is applied in cases when the number of samples is relatively small or when the true distribution is unknown. After about thirty samples, the data should approximate a normal distribution. The central limit theorem is extremely useful in control charting and in the calculation of process capability.

Confidence interval on mean

One of the more useful forms of statistical inference is the estimation of confidence interval on mean, which requires a population sample. This technique can be useful during the measure and analyze stages of DMAIC. The use of this technique assumes that the sample represents the entire population and that it has a normal distribution. Also, the sample should be constant, meaning that it can be assumed to remain relatively stable through time. During the measure stage, an estimation of confidence interval on mean is used to estimate the process average when a process control cannot be set because of a lack of data. This process average is used for baseline estimates. In the analyze stage, an estimation of the confidence interval on mean is used to examine the similarities and differences between the sample means taken during various process conditions.

Process when the historical standard deviation is known
When the historical standard deviation is known, the process of estimating the confidence interval on the mean begins with calculating the average $\bar{X}$ for n sample units. The confidence interval may then be calculated with the following formula: $\bar{X} - Z_{\alpha/2}(\sigma/\sqrt{n}) < \mu < \bar{X} + Z_{\alpha/2}(\sigma/\sqrt{n})$. In this approach, it is assumed that the samples are taken from a population with a normal distribution. Therefore, the z values are calculated according to the confidence level. If the confidence level is 90%, then $\alpha = 0.1$. The confidence interval is two-sided: that is, it extends from one side of the mean to the other. Therefore, the α value is divided in two: $\alpha/2 = 0.05$. The z value, then, can be obtained by referring to a chart of areas under the normal curve.

Process when the historical standard deviation is unknown
In some cases, the historical standard deviation is unknown, and so an alternate method for estimating the confidence interval on the mean must be used. First, one must calculate the average $\bar{X}$ and the sample standard deviation s for n sample units. The confidence interval is calculated with the formula $\bar{X} - t_{\alpha/2,n-1}(s/\sqrt{n}) < \mu < \bar{X} + t_{\alpha/2,n-1}(s/\sqrt{n})$. As with a known historical standard deviation, it is assumed that the samples are taken from a population with a normal distribution. Again, the confidence interval will be two-sided, so confidence level should be divided by two. Confidence interval calculations can be executed in both Minitab and Excel, although in Minitab one must have the raw data in order to proceed.

Interpretation
An estimation of the confidence interval on the mean indicates the percentage of samples that will contain the true population mean, otherwise known as μ (mu). For example, if the confidence limit on the mean is estimated at 97%, one can expect that 97% of samples the confidence interval will include μ. The estimation of the true mean becomes more assured as the number of sampled increases. In other words, the confidence interval and the number of samples are inversely proportionate. This estimation is more powerful when the standard deviation, or σ,

is known. When the standard deviation is unknown, the *t* tables must be used. When the standard deviation is known, the *z* tables may be used.

Confidence interval on proportion

In some cases, analysts will have a solid history of the standard deviation for a given population. In such cases, analysts can estimate the confidence level of the mean at a particular confidence level. This statistical technique can be useful during the measure and analyze stages of DMAIC. As with the confidence interval on mean, the sample being used must represent the entire population, must be constant, and must have a normal distribution. In the measure stage, this technique is useful in situations where limited data exists for the purposes of establishing a process control. In such a case, estimations of the confidence interval on proportion can be used to estimate the average error rates for processes.

Process
To estimate the confidence interval on proportion, begin by calculating the average error rate $\hat{p}$ for *n* sample units. The confidence interval is then calculated with the formula $\hat{p} - Z_{\alpha/2}\sqrt{\frac{\hat{p}(1-\hat{p})}{n}} \leq p \leq \hat{p} + Z_{\alpha/2}\sqrt{\frac{\hat{p}(1-\hat{p})}{n}}$. As with estimate of the confidence interval on proportion, this operation assumes that the samples are taken from a population with a normal distribution. Also, the confidence interval is two-sided, running from one side of the mean to the other. The *z* value can be obtained from a table that outlines areas under the standard normal curve.

Interpretation
The confidence interval on proportion indicates the percentage of samples in which the confidence interval will include the true error rate. For example, if the confidence limit on the error rate is calculated as 90%, it may be assumed that nine out of ten samples will include the true error rate if the confidence interval is reached. As with the interval on the mean, the confidence interval on proportion decreases as the number of samples increases. In other words, when more samples are obtained, fewer values are required to create confidence. The opposite is true, as well: when the number of samples is small, a larger confidence interval is required. Process stability cannot be determined simply by the fact that a particular sample falls within the confidence interval. Process stability must be confirmed with a statistical process control chart.

Sampling methods

Various approaches to sampling exist. Simple random sampling occurs when every unit in the population has the same chance of being selected. When the population is divided into groups and a sample is taken from each of the groups, stratified sampling has occurred. In a systematic sampling program, some method exists regarding the selection of samples. For instance, every third unit might be selected.

In a cluster sampling program, a representative group is selected out of the population, and then a random sample is drawn from that group. This method depends on the ability of the sampler to select a truly representative group. Finally, judgment sampling programs rely on expert opinions in their selection of a sample group. This mode of sampling is appropriate when the samples must have particular characteristics not common to every member of the population.

Distributions

Statistical distributions allow Six Sigma teams to make performance assumptions with a minimum of supporting data. When discrete data is obtained, the binomial and Poisson distributions may be used. When the data is continuous, the normal, exponential, Johnson, and Pearson distributions are applicable. Discrete data is obtained from processes that can be counted. For instance, collections of error data usually will consist of the number of times the error occurred. Continuous data, on the other hand, is derived from measurement. As such, continuous data indicates not just the number of events, but also the extent of each event. Distributions may be useful in the measure, analyze, improve, and control stages of DMAIC. The primary utility of these tools involves determining the characteristics, most notably the sigma level, of processes and resources. Six Sigma professionals also may use these tools to create random data for use during process modeling.

<u>Binomial and Poisson distributions</u>
Binomial distributions are useful when the units in a population exist in only two states. For instance, if the only possible characteristics of a population are "off" and "on," a binomial distribution can be used to estimate the total number of "offs" and "ons" in a population. A binomial distribution only applies when trials are independent and the number of samples in the population is fixed. In a binomial distribution, the distributional parameter is the average proportion. This value is assumed or calculated by dividing the number of sample items that meet the condition by the total number of items in the sample. A Poisson distribution, on the other hand, can guess the number of times a particular condition will occur for a given process or population. The distinguishing feature of the Poisson distribution is its appropriateness for situations in which the targeted condition may occur more than once in each unit. The Poisson distribution accurately estimates the number of events in each sample unit. As with the binomial distribution, the trials be should be independent, and the data should be composed of positive whole numbers. In a Poisson distribution, the distributional parameter is the average number of instances per unit.

<u>Exponential and lognormal distributions</u>
Exponential distributions are used for continuous data, or data obtained by measurement. The most common application for this distribution is in the measurement of event rate, or the frequency with which a particular event occurs. If the event rate essentially is constant, the exponential distribution is appropriate. The distributional parameter is λ (lambda), calculated $1/\mu$, where μ is the interval

between events. Lognormal distributions are appropriate for continuous data that has a fixed lower boundary, usually zero, and no upper boundary. This distribution is used often for reliability data. As with other distributions, a goodness-of-fit test can determine whether a lognormal distribution credibly summarizes the data.

Normal distributions
Normal distributions are used for continuous data that have neither an upper nor a lower boundary. A normal distribution looks like the classic bell curve. For a normal distribution, the average of a sample, $\bar{X}$, is calculated by adding all the measurements and dividing by the total number of measurements, N. The standard deviation of N is calculated with the following formula:

$$s = \frac{\sum_{j=1}^{N} (\bar{X} - X_1)^2}{N}.$$

One must the calculate a z value so this particular standard deviation may be considered a standardized normal distribution with a standard deviation of 1 and a mean of zero. The z value is calculated with $z = \frac{(X - \bar{X})}{s}$. Once this z value is obtained, it is possible to estimate the likelihood of being greater or less than a particular value for x.

Weibull and Johnson distributions
Weibull distributions are appropriate for continuous data with a set lower boundary, usually zero, and no upper boundary. Like the lognormal distribution, the Weibull distribution often applies to reliability data, in which the interval between failures is recorded. A Johnson distribution, on the other hand, is appropriate for continuous data on which neither a normal nor an exponential distribution may be used. Johnson distributions often are useful for data obtained after quality improvement campaigns, because the adjustments to process create non-results. A Johnson distribution assumes that the data represents the process during the period of collection and that one distribution accurately can represent the data. These assumptions are key because they assert that enough data has been collected to make visible any common causes of variation. Johnson distributions are more provisional than others, although any statistical distribution should be taken with a grain of salt.

Parameters of statistical distribution
The four primary parameters of a statistical distribution are central tendency, skewness, standard deviation, and kurtosis. The central tendency is the general trend indicated by the data. In a symmetrical distribution such as the normal distribution, the mean is the best estimate of the central tendency. In an asymmetrical distribution, the median is a more accurate site of the central tendency. The skewness of a distribution is essentially the distance between the average and the mode, or the most-represented data value. A symmetrical distribution has no skew. Standard deviation indicates the average variation of data points from the mean. A measure of standard deviation suggests how close to the

mean each data point likely will be. Finally, kurtosis is the sharpness of the distribution's peak. In a normal distribution, the kurtosis is 1. A distribution with a sharper peak will have a higher value for the kurtosis.

Box-whisker charts

Box-whisker charts are graphs used for the comparison of summary data from numerous data sets. The data sets may be organized by any general principle or characteristic. Box-whisker charts may be used in the analyze and improve stages of DMAIC. During the analyze stage, box-whisker charts may be used to compare the placement and characteristics of services, products, or processes. During the improve stage, box-whisker charts may be used to compare process performance before and after improvement efforts. It should be noted that box-whisker charts do not contain statistical control limits and therefore cannot be used to baseline or set statistical controls for a process. In other words, box-whisker charts are not control charts.

Creation

A box-whisker chart features horizontal and vertical axes. Above each mark on the horizontal axis, a bisected box with lines, or whiskers, will extend from the top and bottom. The upper and lower edges of the box indicate the dimensions of the first and third quartiles of data. The whiskers indicate the upper and lower limits according to special formulae. The lower limit is calculated with the formula Lower Limit = Q1 – 1.5 × (Q3 – Q1). The upper limit is calculated with the formula Upper Limit = Q3 + 1.5 × (Q3 – Q1). Typically, the box and whiskers should be based on quartiles; however, with normal distributions it is also possible to use metrics like mean and standard deviations. For instance, the box could define ±2 standard deviations, and the whiskers could indicate ±4 standard deviations. Some box-whisker charts will include dots beyond the upper and lower limits, indicating the greatest and least data points, respectively. Before creating and interpreting a box-whisker chart, establishing appropriate statistical controls is essential.

Scatter diagrams

A scatter diagram is a simple plot on two axes, useful for investigating the correlation between two variables. Scatter diagrams are used during the analyze stage of DMAIC. The *x*-axis of a scatter diagram measures the independent variable (is the variable manipulated in the experiment) and the *y*-axis measures the dependent variable (the variable not manipulated in the experiment). The general method of an experiment involves making small adjustments to the independent variable and observing the effects on the dependent variable. The independent variable should be manipulated throughout the entire region of interest, so data points achieve sufficient spread on the diagram. Also, the data used on a scatter diagram should be generated especially for that purpose. Experimenters should be cautious when one variable appears to change along with another, since correlation does not imply causation. Perceived correlations suggest a need for further experimentation.

Histograms

A histogram is a tool for presenting data pictorially. It looks like a standard bar graph, except that each bar represents the total number of observations that lie within a range of ranked values. Histograms may be used during the measure and analyze stages of DMAIC. In these stages, histograms are useful for identifying multiple distributions for applying a distribution to capability analysis. Histograms are created by first placing all data in order from least to greatest. The number of bars in a histogram should equal the square root of the total set of data values. The width of each bar is the quotient of the range of data and the number of bars. The range of the data is calculated by subtracting the minimum value from the maximum value. Next, one should determine the number of data observations in each bar. The horizontal axis of the histogram will indicate the data values for each bar, and the vertical axis will indicate the number of observations.

Interpretation

Histograms effectively pinpoint the process location and variation. Histograms also indicate when data is symmetrical or bounded. A symmetrical distribution is characterized by data spread evenly about the histogram's center in an arrangement similar to a bell curve. If the histogram is more skewed, the data is not distributed evenly. For instance, if the data has more than one peak, it may have been obtained from multiple sources. A histogram only indicates the performance of the process as it is being measured. If the sample period was extended, the output would be considerably broader. Also, histograms do not take the sequence of the points into account, so they must be accompanied by measures of statistical process control. It is important to use a control chart to identify statistical control before fitting a distribution.

Gauge repeatability and reproducibility analysis

Gauge repeatability and reproducibility analysis assigns a numerical value to the errors caused by a particular measurement system. Gauge repeatability and reproducibility analysis is used most often during the measure and control stages of DMAIC. In the measure stage, this analysis generally is used to assess the degree to which measurement error contributes to common- and special-cause variation in estimates of process baseline. It also can be used in this stage to confirm gauge discrimination. In the control stage, gauge repeatability and reproducibility analysis is used to evaluate the accuracy of specific measurement systems. The success of an R & R analysis depends on the collection of representative samples. A measurement system cannot be evaluated correctly except by its performance with respect to typical samples.

<u>Process</u>

When analyzing gauge repeatability and reproducibility (R & R), using samples obtained during actual operations is essential. Also, each appraiser should receive the samples in a random order, although someone other than the appraiser should be able to identify the samples. In a standard gauge repeatability and reproducibility analysis, there are three appraisers and ten samples: each appraiser measures each sample three times. However the test is arranged, there should be multiple trials for each sample in order for repeatability to be assessed. While a large sample size is preferable, this analysis can be expensive, which is a limiting factor. Again, it is essential to obtain a representative sample so all the potential sources of variation in the process are evident.

Linearity analysis

Linearity analysis judges the possibility that the bias error found in a particular system of measurement will be present throughout the equipment's entire operating range. It is important to know whether a measurement system can be trusted for large as well as small values. Linearity analysis often is used during the measure stage of DMAIC. In this stage, linearity analysis is useful for assessing the accuracy of a measurement system within the range of values likely to be observed during the process. The standard procedure for analyzing linearity was established by the Automotive Industry Action Group. The first step selecting multiple parts to examine throughout the operating range. A reference value should be obtained with precise equipment. The next step is having different employees measure the parts throughout the range with the intended measurement system. The average of these measurements should be found, and then the bias can be calculated by subtracting the average measurement from the reference value. This data then should be depicted on a scatter diagram. The adequacy of the measurement system is assessed using R^2, the coefficient of determination. A value of greater than 70% is acceptable in most cases.

Process capability index

A process capability index quantifies the ability of a process to meet the expectations of customers and other stakeholders. This index usually is converted into a standard deviation or estimate of defects per million opportunities. Process capability indices typically are used during the measure, improve, and control stages of DMAIC. In the measure stage, process capability indices can create a baseline estimate for a controlled process. During the improve stage, a process capability index can confirm process improvements and assure the team that the process is in statistical control. In the control stage, these indices are used to monitor processes, generally to confirm that they remain in a state of statistical control. For all of these uses, the process must be in statistical control. Otherwise, measures of process capability cannot be trusted. If the process has both upper and lower specifications, the statistics C_p and C_{pk} can be used. If only one of the specifications is known, C_{pk} must be used.

- 39 -

Creation

Before process capability can be calculated, it is necessary to use a control chart to determine the stability of the process. The capability indices for a normal distribution are calculated $C_p = \frac{\text{high spec} - \text{low spec}}{6\sigma_x}$, $C_{pk} = \min(Cp_l, Cp_u)$, and $C_{pm} = \frac{C_p}{\sqrt{1 + \frac{(\bar{\bar{x}} - T)^2}{\sigma_{\bar{x}}^2}}}$. In these equations, $\bar{\bar{x}}$ is the grand average, T is the process target,

and σ_x is process sigma. If the subgroup size is 1, process sigma is calculated according to the moving-range statistic. If the subgroup size is greater than 1, the process sigma is calculated with the subgroup sigma statistic.

$$C_p = \frac{Z_L}{3} \qquad\qquad Cp_u = \frac{Z_u}{3} \qquad\qquad Z_l = \frac{\bar{\bar{x}} - \text{low spec}}{\sigma_x} \qquad\qquad Z_u = \frac{\text{high spec} - \bar{\bar{x}}}{\sigma_x}$$

The capability indices for non-normal distributions are calculated with $C_p = \frac{\text{high spec} - \text{low spec}}{\text{ordinate}_{0.99865} - \text{ordinate}_{0.00135}}$, $Z_l = |Z_{\text{normal},p}|$, and $Z_u = |Z_{\text{normal},1-p}|$. In these equations, ordinate$_{0.99865}$ and ordinate$_{0.00135}$ are the z values for the non-normal distribution curve at 99.865 and 0.135. Also, $Z_{\text{normal},p}$ and $Z_{\text{normal},1-p}$ are the z values of the normal cumulative distribution curve at the p and $1 - p$ percentage points, respectively.

Interpretation

A process capability index is influenced heavily by the distribution assumptions. If the value of C_p (the ratio of tolerance to process variation) is 1, then tolerance and process variation are equal. If the value of C_p is less than one, then the allowable variation is less than the process variation, which means that the normal amount of variation could be too much. This is a bad situation. When C_{pk} is used, it is possible to obtain information about the process variation and location and their relation to the requirements. The statistic C_{pm} is much like C_{pk}, but it also considers the relation between process average and a target value. If these values are the same, then C_{pm} and C_{pk} are equal.

Process performance indices

A process performance index determines whether a particular batch of materials will be satisfactory to customers. That its scope is limited to a single batch distinguishes the process performance index from the process capability index. Process performance indices are used most often in the measure stage of DMAIC. In this stage, they are used to create process baseline estimates for uncontrolled processes. To do so, however, the sample must be quite largein order to assess any variations in the batch. In most cases, statistical process controls are preferred over process performance indices. However, sometimes statistical process controls will not be possible, whether because the process lacks statistical control or because there is insufficient data.

Creation

If the batch sample has both upper and lower specifications, then the P_p statistic may be used. When only one of the specifications is present, the P_{pk} statistic can be used. The performance indices for normal distributions are calculated $P_p = \frac{\text{high spec}-\text{low spec}}{6\sigma_x}$, $P_{pk} = \min(Pp_l, Pp_u)$, and $p_{pm} = \frac{p_p}{\sqrt{1+\frac{(\bar{\bar{x}}-T)^2}{\sigma_x^2}}}$. In these equations, $\bar{\bar{x}}$ is the grand average, T is the process target, and σ_x is the sample sigma.

$$P_{pl} = \frac{Z_l}{3} \qquad P_{pu} = \frac{Z_u}{3} \qquad Z_l = \frac{\bar{\bar{x}}-\text{low spec}}{\sigma_x} \qquad Z_u = \frac{\text{high spec}-\bar{\bar{x}}}{\sigma_x}$$

When the distributions are non-normal, performance indices are calculated as $C_p = \frac{\text{high spec}-\text{low spec}}{\text{ordinate}_{0.99865}-\text{ordinate}_{0.00135}}$, $Z_l = |Z_{\text{normal},p}|$, and $Z_u = |Z_{\text{normal},1-p}|$. In these equations, $\text{ordinate}_{0.99865}$ and $\text{ordinate}_{0.00135}$ are the z values for the non-normal distribution curve at 99.865 and 0.135. Also, $Z_{\text{normal},p}$ and $Z_{\text{normal}, 1 - p}$ are the z values of the normal cumulative distribution curve at the p and $1 - p$ percentage points.

Interpretation

Unlike statistical control charts, process performance indices cannot be used to predict future performance. A measure of process performance incorporates sample sigma (that is, standard deviation), so it cannot suggest process capability for the future. Although using capability indices generally is better, when a process is in statistical control the calculation of process performance indices will be remarkably similar to process capability indices. If the process performance indices have values less than 1, then tolerance (variation that can be allowed) is less than the variation in the sample. If the value is 1, then the variation in the sample is exactly the same as the tolerance. The best result is to have process performance indice values of greater than 1, indicating that the sample variation is less than the allowable variation.

Analyze

Primary objectives of the analyze stage

In the analyze stage of DMAIC, the Six Sigma team will focus on analyzing the sources of variation in the target process. This analysis may require the use of sophisticated statistical tools. The team also will analyze the value stream. The value stream is the set of activities that create value for the customer. During the analyze stage, the team will identify the process drivers, which are the activities that exert a significant influence on the results of processes. Obviously, the intention of the Six Sigma efforts will be to enhance those activities that add value and to eliminate those activities that take up time and resources without adding much value. The value stream only includes those activities necessary for the creation of the product or service. The judgment of value should be from the perspective of the customer rather than from the perspective of stakeholders within the company.

Multi-vari plots

Multi-vari plots are effective tools for assessing the variation within samples or within particular parts. Multi-vari plots also can be used to analyze variation over time or between different batches. Multi-vari plots are used during the analyze stage of DMAIC. In this stage, they are primarily used to isolate the causes of variation and to obtain more information about the interactions among factors. The first step in constructing a multi-vari plot is determining the system for gathering data. This data should then be placed on a plot, with each sample unit represented by a different symbol. The length of each symbol will indicate the variation within the sample. The point of a multi-vari plot is to isolate the causes of variation. However, this tool is not a control chart, so it will not indicate whether the process is unstable from a statistical perspective.

Equality-of-variance tests

Equality-of-variance tests determine whether a similar degree of variation exists in particular subsets of data. This question is important because an effective analysis of variance cannot be performed unless equal variance has been established. Equality-of-variance tests are used primarily during the analyze and improve stages. During these stages, the tests are useful for assessing the observed data obtained during an analysis of variance. Equality-of-variance tests also may be used after regression analysis in order to assess the residuals. A few different forms of this test exist. The most typical statistical test used to measure equality of variance is the Bartlett, although versions also are offered on Levene and Minitab. The Levene test is recommended in situations where non-normality is a strong possibility.

The most common test for equality of variance is the Bartlett, the appropriate test when the regression residuals are expected to follow a normal distribution. In the Bartlett test, the equality of the treatment variances is compared with the possibility that one variance is unequal to the others. The null hypothesis of the test holds that the subsets have equal variances, which is expressed as $H_o: \sigma^2{}_1 = \sigma^2{}_1 = \sigma^2{}_2 = \cdots = \sigma^2{}_a$, where a is the set of experimental conditions. If the null hypothesis is false, then at least one of the subsets must have an unequal variance. In order to assess the variance at each position, one must have more than one sample from each test condition. When non-normal variance is apparent, the variable in question can be transformed, which will mitigate its effect.

Autocorrelation charts

Autocorrelation charts, otherwise known as the autocorrelation function (ACF), are used to determine the degree to which current data depends on previously gathered data. This is accomplished by automatically examining multiple observations of a particular characteristic with an eye toward possible correlations. This operation is similar to the scatter diagram, except the latter identifies correlations between different characteristics. Autocorrelation charts are useful during the measure, analyze, and control stages. In the measure stage, these charts may be used to gather information about processes, including their effects on baseline data. During the analyze stage, autocorrelation charts are used to investigate the regression residuals, namely to test for independence. In the control stage, autocorrelation charts are used to develop a strategy that takes into account a process' serial dependence.

Process
The first step of the autocorrelation function is testing for autocorrelations between each of the isolated observations. Each step will be considered in relation to the steps immediately before and after it. This consideration is called the lag 1 autocorrelation. There also will be autocorrelations for distances. For example, the lag 3 autocorrelation will consider the relations between the first and fourth observations, second and fifth observations, and so on. The general recommendation suggests testing for autocorrelations from lag 1 to lag $n/4$, where n is the total number of observations. The estimation of the autocorrelation function for lag m is as follows: $r_m = \frac{\sum_{i=1}^{n-m}(X_i - \bar{X})(X_{i+m} - \bar{X})}{\sum_{i=1}^{n}(X_i - \bar{X})^2}$, where n is the total number of observations and $\bar{X}$ is the average of these observations.

Process partial autocorrelation
The formula for estimating the partial autocorrelation function is $\Phi_{mm} = \frac{r_m - \sum_{j=1}^{n-m}\Phi_{m-1,j}r_{m-1}}{1 - \sum_{j=1}^{m-1}\Phi_{m-i,j}r_j}$, for a given lag of m. In this formula, the autocorrelation function is r_m. The significance limits for both the autocorrelation function and the partial autocorrelation function (if the true population of the ACF or PACF is zero) is

calculated at the stated significance level. However, if the true population of the autocorrelation function or partial autocorrelation function is larger, then the significance limit must be determined with $r, \Phi = \pm \left(\frac{k}{\sqrt{n}} \right)$, in which n is the number of observations and k is the ordinate of the normal distribution at the stated significance level.

Interpretation of autocorrelation charts

When interpreting an autocorrelation chart, one should be aware of phenomena that might produce false correlation. For instance, sometimes autocorrelation will be significant only at adjacent data points, where the lag is very low. To diminish this autocorrelation, one should increase the time between data point collection. Another source of false correlation emerges with sampling from several different streams in a process. Sometimes large autocorrelations for smaller lags can influence larger lags. For example, if a strong correlation exists between observation four and observation five and another strong correlation exists between observation five and observation six, observation four and observation six may appear correlated even when no such correlation actually exists. This illusion can be diminished by using the partial autocorrelation function. In any case, autocorrelation functions and partial autocorrelation functions range from -1 to 1. The farther away the value is from zero, the stronger the correlation.

Regression analysis

Regression analysis is a system for identifying when independent variables are influenced by one or more dependent variables. Regression analysis may be used during the measure, analyze, and improve stages of DMAIC. In the measure stage, regression analysis is used to evaluate the degree to which a measurement system is linear. During the analyze stage, regression analysis can be used to explore the connections between metrics and process factors. In the improve stage, regression analysis is useful for confirming these connections after improvements have been implemented. A scatter diagram often is interpreted with a simple linear regression analysis. If more than one factor influences the value of the independent variable, then multiple regression is necessary.

Simple linear regression

A simple linear regression tries to orient data points around a single straight line. In mathematics, the equation for this line is written $y = mx + b$, where y is the dependent variable, m is the slope, x is the independent variable, and b is the point along the y-axis where $x = 0$ (often referred to as the y-intercept). This is known as slope-intercept form. In Six Sigma, however, it is more common to see the formula expressed $Y = \beta_0 + \beta_1 X +$ error, where β_0 is the estimation of the intercept and β_1 is the regression line's slope. The values for intercept and slope typically are estimated according to the method of least squares, in which the line is drawn with a minimal squared distance to each data point. The statistical equation for a simple linear regression includes the word *error* as an acknowledgement that every set of data points will have some inaccuracies.

First-order model of multiple regression

If more than one factor influences a dependent variable, a multiple regression must be used. A multiple regression takes into account the interactions between these multiple factors. In a first-order model, the value of the dependent variable is based on the influence of each factor by itself, as well as each possible combination of two factors. Whatever error exists in the model is assumed to be the same for all factors and combinations of factors. A first-order multiple regression usually will produce an essentially straight line over small regions, so it can be useful when only targeted data is needed. Examined from a more distant perspective, however, the model will appear as a linear regression for which the plane has been curved or twisted. This flexing of the plane is caused by the influence of interacting factors.

Higher-order models of multiple regression

When more complex analysis is required for a process in which more than one factor influences a dependent variable, a higher-order model of multiple regression must be performed. For instance, a higher-order multiple regression can include squares and cubes of the values, which will produce a response surface with definable peaks and valleys. A higher-order multiple regression is valuable only if exhaustive experiments already have been performed on the main effects. Multiple regression models with higher orders are useful for mapping smaller regions, in particular peaks, valleys, and minimaxes (intersections between the minimum for one factor and the maximum for another). Higher-order multiple regression models also are good at defining the area that surrounds a stationary point. In Six Sigma, these models often are used to evaluate how current operating parameters influence the response.

Residuals analysis

Residuals are the differences between a response's observed value and a regression model's predicted value for that response. A residuals analysis of a regression model will reveal any unusual patterns that could suggest error in the model. In statistical terms, this is expressed $e_i = y_i - \hat{y}_i$. Statistical software programs such as Excel will calculate a standardized residual $e_i/\sqrt{s^2}$, such that the variance is set to 1. This makes outliers more obvious. Perhaps the most common technique of residuals analysis is the normality test, in which the randomness of error is tested by creating a distribution of the residuals. If the error truly is random, then the residuals should follow a normal distribution with a mean of zero. Residuals also can be used on a scatter diagram to assess the independence of a variable.

NVA activities in the analyze stage of DMAIC

Identification
Six Sigma teams use tools such as matrix diagrams and quality function deployment efforts to identify non-value-added activities. As always, the question of value should be considered from the customer's perspective. If an activity does not create something for which a customer would be willing to pay, it likely does not add value. One common form of NVA activity is improper or unsuccessful designs. When a business spends time and effort designing products or services that the customer ultimately rejects, then the business has failed to add value. If a business process contains some unnecessary or redundant steps, these steps are classified as NVA activities. Any work that does not translate into a product or service for the customer is considered NVA. For instance, inventory reorganization provides nothing to the customer, although it may be necessary at times. Any unnecessary transport of people or resources is considered NVA activity.

Elimination
In the analyze stage of DMAIC, the Six Sigma team will be alert to non-value-added activities that expand cycle time. Non-value-added activities (NVA) create nothing for which a customer would be willing to pay. One common example of an NVA activity that expands cycle time is an authorization requirement. Cycle time extends unnecessarily when an employee must receive permission from his or her superior before moving on to the next step of a processThis unnecessary extension is true especially when the task has become rote, and authorization is a meaningless formality. Some businesses have implemented checklists requiring employees to complete paperwork at every step in a process. These checklists often are unnecessary and time-consuming.

Hypothesis testing

Hypothesis testing establishes a degree of confidence and then compares a sample statistic against a historical value or another sample statistic. In other words, hypothesis testing allows one to make statistical inferences about the characteristics of a population. This sort of testing is useful for distinguishing the factors that contribute to variation in data. Primarily, this type of testing is used during designed experiments and regression analysis. Hypothesis testing often is performed during the analyze and improve stages of DMAIC. In the improve stage, its primary function is comparing the averages of improved processes with baseline estimates. In order to perform hypothesis testing, the population must be assumed constant and homogenous. Also, that samples are random and representative must be assumed.

Process
The first step in hypothesis testing is stating the null hypothesis, H_0. In most cases, the null hypothesis represents the value that the test aspires to prove. Since a hypothesis test only can reject the null hypothesis or fail to reject it, in some cases framing the null hypothesis as something to be disproved makes more sense. The

next step in hypothesis testing is defining the alternative hypothesis (H_1). The alternative hypothesis should cover all of the area excluded from the null hypothesis. The third step is either setting a value for p or selecting a significance level (α). The significance level is the chance of incorrectly rejecting a true hypothesis in what is known as a Type 1 error. Generally, it is considered better to set a p value because this allows more freedom for adjustment later in the experiment. Next, samples are collected and statistics are calculated. The final step in hypothesis testing is drawing a conclusion.

Interpretation

Interpreting a hypothesis test is simple. If the calculated statistic is larger than the critical value of the test statistic for the given level of significance, then the null hypothesis must be rejected. If the critical value of the test statistic is larger, then the null hypothesis is not rejected. Software programs such as Excel or Minitab can use the calculated p value to indicate whether the obtained results are appropriate, assuming that the null hypothesis is true. If the p value is small, then the chances of obtaining results similar to those gathered during the experiment are so small that the null hypothesis should be rejected. If the null hypothesis is not rejected, the experiment is said to have reached a weak conclusion, because the means may or may not be equal. When the null hypothesis is confirmed, however, the experiment is said to have produced a strong conclusion, or a definitive statement that the means are not equal.

Nonparametric tests on equality of means

Nonparametric tests occasionally are used in place of traditional hypothesis tests for the equality of two means. These tests are more effective when the assumptions associated with common statistical distributions cannot be met. Nonparametric tests are used during the analyze and improve stages of DMAIC. In the analyze stage, nonparametric tests are used to compare the means from samples with different conditions. In the improve stage, they are used to assess whether process averages have been improved over baseline estimates after the implementation of changes. These tests do not require statistical normality or any other quality in order to be valid. One disadvantage of this form of testing is its requirement of a larger sample size. Nonparametric tests are available in every version of statistical software.

Creation and interpretation

For a nonparametric test on the equality of means, the null hypothesis H_0 will be that population 1's median is equal to population 2's median. The alternative hypothesis H_1, then, is that population 1's median does not equal population 2's median. Median is preferable to mean in these tests because it indicates central tendency regardless of distribution. The next step in the test involves declaring a significance level or p value. After samples have been collected, the probability of Type II error can be assessed. Upon completing the test, it is possible to compare the calculated statistics with a test statistic. The null hypothesis is rejected if the calculated statistic is greater than the critical value of the test statistic. If the calculated statistic does not exceed the critical value of the test statistic, then the null hypothesis cannot be rejected. Nonetheless, this rejection does not imply confirmation of the null hypothesis.

ANOVA

An analysis of variance (ANOVA) is a table that depicts the sum-of-squares variance that can be credited to a particular source, the sum of the squares that can be credited to error, and the total sum of squares from the data. This table includes F statistics related to the significance of the source relative to the error. An analysis of variance may be performed during the measure or analyze stages of DMAIC. During the measure stage, analysis of variance is used to identify the origins of errors in measurement. This analysis is useful especially for processes that damage or diminish the resources involved, such that a repeatability and reproducibility (R & R) is not possible. In the analyze stage, analysis of variance can be used to gather information about the statistical significance of a regression models. Six Sigma teams often will use ANOVA in this manner to pinpoint possible process drivers. Another use of analysis of variance in the analyze stage is to identify differences between data subsets with the intention of identifying the causes of variation within a process.

In an analysis of variance, variation within each subgroup is compared to the variation found between different subgroups. The variation within each subgroup is found by sampling from the subgroup repeatedly. The variation between different subgroups is found by analyzing the essential differences between the averages of each subgroup. Analysis of variance begins with the null hypothesis, that all subgroup averages are equal. Then, the F statistic is used to compare the average variation between subsets, known as the mean square treatment, with the sun of the squares of the residuals, known as the mean square error. An F test assumes that subsets have a normal distribution and equal variance. If the p value for the F test is less than 0.05, then the null hypothesis can be rejected. This suggests that one or more of the subset averages is different.

Goodness-of-fit tests

A number of useful goodness-of-fit tests measure the validity of statistical assessment. In other words, these tests indicate whether a chosen statistical test provide an accurate and relevant measure. Goodness-of-fit tests may be used during the measure, analyze, improve, and control stages of DMAIC. During these stages, the tests are used to confirm a distribution. This confirmation enables the team to assume the validity of confidence tests, statistical control charts, hypothesis tests, and other tests. Some of the most common goodness-of fit tests are the chi-square, Anderson-Darling, and Kolmogorov-Smirnov (K-S). The simplest of these tests is the chi-square, which can be explained and run without the need for special software. The Anderson-Darling and Kolmogorov-Smirnov tests are more specific, however, and provide better results when used appropriately.

Creation and interpretation

Most experts agree that a distributional fit cannot be tested properly without at least two hundred data points. However, if a process is not in statistical control, no distribution will fit its data points. In the Kolmogorov-Smirnov test, the actual data points generally will vary slightly from the curve that best charts their values. This difference should decrease as the number of data points rises. The K-S test essentially checks to see if this inverse relationship exists. The Anderson-Darling test, on the other hand, emphasizes the data obtained at the extreme ends of the distribution. In the assessment of a normal distribution, the mean should be approximately the value of the line as it passes through the 50th percentile. If too much data falls in the tails of the distribution, then there will be an abundance of points above the confidence interval on the left side and below the confidence interval on the right. Goodness-of-fit tests have a null hypothesis that the data follows the distribution in question. The measure of this fit is known as the p value. Typically, a larger p value indicates better fit.

Batching

Disadvantages

Batching is a traditional method of reducing waste. When work is batched, a specialized group of employees gathers a large number of essentially identical tasks and performs them all at the same time. The group of similar tasks is known as a batch. Throughout most of the modern era of organizational management, batching was considered to make processes more efficient. However, research conducted during Six Sigma efforts has revealed that batching often increases overall cycle time. When process tasks are divided into batches, the time required to perform them clearly is shorter. However, batching creates delays at the beginning and end of the activity. The team must wait for a number of tasks to arrive in the "in tray" before beginning. This wait creates unnecessary lag time. Also, batching typically means that the entire collection of materials does not move on to the next step of the process until everyone has been subjected to the batched step. A product or service may be ready to move on for quite a long time, but may have to wait until the other products or services have been processed.

Benefits

In some cases, batching is a good strategy for processing materials or performing activities. For instance, if the time required to set up the equipment for a particular activity is significant, performing the activity in batches may be more efficient. As an example, consider the process of making soup from scratch. Even if you are making soup only for yourself, you likely will make much more soup than you can eat in a single sitting, because the time required to gather and manipulate the ingredients is too long to spend on one serving. Without even thinking about it, most people recognize that cooking a large pot of soup is more sensible. Another scenario in which batching makes sense is when the cost of moving materials is large. This scenario occurs often in the shipping of small items. For instance, a business may

- 49 -

need only a small number of staples every week, but the cost of shipping office supplies is high enough to suggest that the business should buy large batches of supplies infrequently rather than a small amount of supplies more often.

Lean metric velocity

Velocity, in lean management, is a metric that indicates the rate at which value is added during a process phase. The calculation of the lean metric velocity is useful during the analyze stage of DMAIC, where it can place cycle time improvement opportunities in order of importance. The basic formula for the calculation of velocity requires dividing the number of value-added steps by the process lead time. Process lead time is calculated according to Little's law, by dividing the number of items in the process by the number of times the process is completed every hour. Of course, objective figures for these variables are not always readily available. Often, initiating a process observation log is helpful before attempting to calculate velocity.

Calculating process velocity

The first step in the calculation of process velocity requires categorizing every task in the process as value-added, non-value-added but necessary (NVA type 1), or non-value-added and unnecessary (NVA type 2). The next step involves measuring the physical distance between the sites of each successive task. Next, the team will use a control chart to predict the average time required to complete each process task. Then the team will use a control chart to estimate the amount of time a customer or employee must wait before beginning each successive step in the process. At this time, the team also should estimate the number of items in each queue. Again, the control chart is the most valuable tool for this purpose. The averages of all these measurements can be added together to obtain the total number of items in the process and the number of times the process is completed each hour. This is all the information required to calculate process lead time. Velocity is calculated by dividing the number of value-added steps by the process lead time.

Usage of velocity data

The calculation of velocity indicates the degree to which a process responds to customer demands. If there is less work in progress, lead times are shorter and velocity is greater. If the lead times are longer, then velocity is slower. When velocity is slow, the business cannot respond quickly to new orders from customers. For example, if an auto body shop takes a long time to finish working on existing projects, it cannot take on new projects. If the cashier at a grocery store works slowly, the line at his or her aisle likely will grow. The formula for process velocity (number of value-added steps divided by process lead time) suggests a couple of approaches for increasing velocity. Either the amount of work in progress can be reduced or the number of completed processes per hour can be increased. Analysis of process efficiency will indicate which of these strategies is appropriate.

Setup time

As part of their efforts to reduce cycle time, businesses often will target the time required to set up and prepare for activities. Six Sigma defines setup time as the interval between the completion of the last item in the sequence and the beginning of the next item. Setup time consists of four components: preparation, replacement, location, and adjustment. Preparation is the set of tasks necessary to gather all of the materials and people for the activity. Replacement is the set of tasks required to adjust and reconfigure equipment before the next item can be processed. For instance, a printer occasionally will need a new batch of paper loaded before it can continue operation. Location, with regard to NVA activities, refers to the positioning or moving tasks that must be completed between iterations of a process. Adjustment is the set of monitoring or fine-tuning tasks that must be performed between iterations to ensure correct performance of a process.

Reducing preparation time

Preparation time is considered a non-value-added activity and therefore should be reduced as much as possible. Preparation is defined as the set of tasks required to collect and store materials and resources before a process can begin. As such, this set of tasks could refer to the collection of resources from a warehouse or the loading of a computer program. In any case, a few common strategies in Six Sigma reduce preparation time. One of these strategies involves keeping all supplies and equipment as close as possible to the workstation, so employees do not waste time in transit. Another strategy for reducing preparation time groups employees from different departments in work cells. In a work cell, each employee is trained and responsible for a different part of the process. Therefore, the entire operation can be completed without moving the work-in-progress. A final strategy for reducing preparation time is leaving equipment on and ready to go even when not in use.

Reducing time spent on relocation and replacement

Six Sigma professionals view moving and replacing equipment and resources prior to a process as non-value-added activities, which therefore should be minimized. One strategy for reducing time lost due to location issues is standardizing setups. For instance, if a bakery produces a number of different goods, baking them at many different temperatures is inefficient. As much as possible, the bakery should keep the oven at the same temperature and instead vary the amount of time each item bakes. A good strategy for reducing replacement tasks is simplifying the setup protocol, altogether. Too often, businesses create elaborate setup checklists appropriate for new employees but unnecessary for employees familiar with their work. One way to simplify setups is by redesigning fixtures. In addition, having a standard setup procedure for all the members of a product family is helpful.

Reducing adjustment time

As much as possible, Six Sigma professionals reduce the time spent making minor adjustments to equipment and resources before each process iteration. The best way to limit adjustment is to establish good process controls. When a process can be repeated many times in a row in exactly the same way, it will require less adjustment. However, this arrangement may require a fundamental redesign of the process. Six Sigma professionals typically use statistical process control charts and designed experiments to identify those areas of the process that necessitate adjustment. The project efforts then will focus on eliminating or reducing these factors. As always, ensuring that the process components being targeted are on the critical path is essential. If process components being targeted are not on the critical path, then modifications will be pointless.

Value of reducing movement and physical space in processes

The analysis stage of DMAIC often reveals that much time is lost simply moving from one work site to another. Indeed, the most effective strategy for reducing cycle time often involves consolidating the area in which a task is performed. This consolidation enables all the stakeholders in a process to perform their jobs with a minimum of waiting and unnecessary energy expenditure. One common approach to reducing wasteful movement requires grouping employees in multi-function rather than single-function departments. An employee group could include representatives from all of the departments required for the process. When possible, employees can be cross-trained so they are capable of performing several different tasks within a complete process. This practice helps stave off boredom and allows employees to replace one another without interruption of work flow. Businesses that reduce unnecessary movement generally spend less on overhead.

Improve and Control

Basic objectives of the improve stage

The improve stage of DMAIC occurs when all of the hard work of the preceding sections finally is applied to processes. The first major objective of the improve stage is to set the new process operating conditions. These conditions are based on the experimentation and analysis of the measure and analyze phases. The next objective of the improve stage is to identify and address the failure modes for the new processes. Assessing and predicting the benefits of the proposed solution also is appropriate. Before making massive changes, the Six Sigma team should be able to guess how positive the results of these solutions will be. The final objective of the improve stage is to implement and confirm process improvements, the moment when the predictions developed during the preceding sections finally are tested against reality.

Factorial designs

Factorial designs are used in the majority of experiments. They may be either complete factorial designs or fractional factorial designs. Factorial designs are useful primarily during the analyze and improve stages of DMAIC. In the analyze stage, fractional factorial designs are used to identify process drivers and sources of variation. In the improve stage, fractional factorial designs are used along with center points to estimate the effects of curvature. A complete factorial design can estimate the characteristics and interactions of all the factors in an experiment. Complete factorial designs analyze the interactions of more than two factors at a time. A fractional factorial design, on the other hand, only looks at the interactions between two factors at a time. Interactions between more than two factors are known as higher-order interactions. Because a fractional factorial design ignores these interactions, it can be performed more quickly.

Complete factorial designs
The number of runs required for a complete factorial design is calculated by raising the number of levels for each factor to the power equal to the number of factors. For instance, if each factor has three levels and there are four factors, the number of required runs will be $3^4 = 81$. The factorial design will look like a standard table, with each row representing a different configuration of the factors. Since the number of factors exists in an exponential relationship to the levels for each factor, a small increase in the number of factors will result in a huge increase in the number of required runs. For this reason, complete factorial designs quickly can become unwieldy and inefficient. It is often better to begin with a fractional factorial design to identify multi-factor interactions that require more study. Complete factorial designs are seldom used in the business world.

Fractional factorial designs

Fractional factorial designs restrict their focus to the interactions between pairs of factors. They get away with this through a process called aliasing, in which interactions of more than two factors are represented as a single new actor. For instance, a factorial design with three factors will not consider the interaction between factors 1, 2, and 3, but instead will create a new factor (4) representative of this interaction. This enables the factorial design to be comprehensive with far fewer runs. The only problem with this approach is that the effects of factor 4 cannot be estimated independent of the interactions of factors 1, 2, and 3. This is referred to as confounded data. Fractional factorial designs are good for quickly identifying factor interactions that should receive more attention in subsequent experiments.

Response surface analysis

Response surface analysis is a set of techniques for calculating the best response value. Best response value may refer to the best possible result of an industrial process or the best possible admixture of employees for a service response. Response surface analysis is used only during the improve stage of DMAIC. Here, it maps the response surface so the effects of varying certain factors can be predicted. Response surface analysis also is used in the improve stage to find the operating conditions that produce the desired specifications. In general, though, response surface analysis is used to achieve the best possible settings for processes and products. Response surface analysis cannot be begun until a first-order regression model has been created from the critical set of significant factors. The Six Sigma team will use screening designs to develop the critical set of significant factors.

Process

Response surface analysis, as it is typically practiced, has three phases, 0 through 2. Phase 0 is considered a prerequisite phase. In this phase, the team uses screening designs to create a critical set of significant factors. Then, a first-order regression model is created. In phase 1 of response surface analysis, the team will use the steepest ascent methodology to define the operating region at present and identify the direction of maximum response. The first-order regression model created during phase 0 can be very useful at this point, because its scale is great enough to ensure that the data points are affected by first-order effects. Phase 2 of response surface analysis is the application of ridge analysis and a second-order model to locate the optimal conditions at stationary points in a small region. In response surface analysis, a stationary point is defined as anywhere that the slope of the second-order response surface model is zero for each of the factors. Stationary points may be a maximum value, a minimum value, or a "mini-max" value, which is the highest or lowest point in a saddle curve. If the stationary point is significantly outside the data range, it may be used only to obtain direction.

- 54 -

Steepest ascent methodology in phase 1

Phase 1 of response surface analysis is the application of steepest ascent methodology to a first-order regression model. Data points are collected along the steepest path beginning with the design center, or the spot where $(x_1, x_2) = (0, 0)$. The design center is the first test condition. The steepest ascent is determined by moving β_1 coded units in the x_1 direction for every β_2 coded units in the x_2 direction, where β_1 and β_2 are the coefficients of the x_1 and x_2 terms, respectively. If the changes are sufficiently small, then obtaining a good picture of the response will be possible. Given a specific change in uncoded units for x_1, it will be possible to obtain values for x_2, β_1, and β_2. It also is possible to determine the path of steepest ascent relative to the physical limitations of the system, such as if either x_1 or x_2 cannot proceed beyond a certain point. The local maximum conditions are determined by looking for the point at which the response begins to diminish. Once the local maximum condition has been determined, another experiment is run near this point to obtain a first-order model with centerpoint(s).

Ridge analysis techniques in phase 2

After a first-order model has been conducted near the maximum at the end of phase 1, there should be several redundant runs to estimate lack of fit. When the lack of fit is insignificant, a new path of steepest ascent may be found by adjusting the intervals, starting point, or direction. If the lack of fit is significant and there is curvature, the point likely is close to a maximum, minimum, or mini-max. At this juncture it now is time to begin phase 2 of the response surface analysis: ridge analysis. In this process, a second-order regression model is generated with a central composite design near the optimum. The next step is to create response surface and contour plots for each two factors. Then, identify the stationary point in the response surface and contour plots. Next, predict the response at the optimum using the second-order regression model. Finally, verify the model by gathering new data in the region around the optimum.

Desirability function

For some processes, attaining optimal performance relative to multiple responses may be possible. Response surface analysis can accomplish this goal with overlaid contour plots or desirability functions. The desirability function is an analytical tool for finding the shared optimal point of multiple functions. To perform the desirability function, one must first define each optimal value as a minimum, maximum, or specified target. The degree to which each response obtains its optimum condition is indicated with a d, and the composite of these responses is designated as D, which is calculated as the geometric mean of each response desirability function: $D = (d_1 \times d_2 \times d_3 \times \uparrow \times d_m)^{1/m}$. This composite value is maximized in each case so d values near the maximum of 1 suggest that all responses are within the desirable range at the same time.

Manipulating response and calculating weights in phase 2

If the intention of using the desirability function is to minimize the response, then there must be a specified target value and an upper boundary. The desired value is

- 55 -

then calculated $d = \left(\frac{\text{response} - \text{upper boundary}}{\text{target} - \text{upper boundary}}\right)^s$. If the intention of using the desirability function is to maximize the response, then there must be a specified target value and a lower boundary. The desired value is then calculated $d = \left(\frac{\text{response} - \text{lower boundary}}{\text{target} - \text{lower boundary}}\right)^s$. If the intention of using the desirability function is to achieve a target value, then that value and the upper and lower boundaries must be defined. If the response falls between the upper boundary and the target, the desirability function should be calculated as in cases where the intention is to minimize the response. If the response falls between the lower boundary and the target, the desirability function should be calculated as in cases where the intention is to maximize the response. The values for the s and t weights depend on the relative emphasis on the target and the boundary. If the target and boundary are valued equally, then the s and t weights are 1. If the target is more important, then s and t weights can be between 1 and 10. If the boundary is more important, the s and t weights can be between 0.1 and 1.

Interpretation
Response surface analysis generates charts that can be subjected to analysis of variance. For instance, the F statistic can be used to compare the sum of squares variation caused by pure error with the sum of squares variation caused by curvature. If the curvature is significant, the point likely is close to a local maximum, minimum, or mini-max (that is, a stationary point). If the stationary point falls outside the experimental region, then new data must be required so the region can be enlarged. If this is impossible because the data point falls in a region that would be impossible to reproduce, then constrained optimization should be applied to the steepest ascent methodology. If the stationary point is determined to be a mini-max, then constrained optimization techniques must be applied to the steepest ascent methodology. The full results then can be analyzed after axial points are added to the design at the new centerpoint. These axial points are placed on the design at places where they will achieve rotatable orthogonal design. Again, it is necessary to collect new data around the optimal point for the purpose of verification.

Contour plots

Contour plots are composed of groups of curves. Each of these curves is assigned a constant value according to a fitted response. The path of each of these curves relates to values that have been separated at regular intervals. Any additional factors are placed on the chart according to their mean or some other value. Contour plots are used typically during the improve stage of DMAIC. Specifically, they are used in response surface analysis to estimate the maximum and minimum responses associated with particular ranges of data. If there are only first-order main effects, the contour plot will have parallel lines separated from one another by equal distances. Whenever interactions occur between the responses, the contour lines curve.

Interaction plots

Interaction plots illustrate the interrelationships of three parameters. In most cases, these parameters are two factors and one response. Interaction plots are used during the analyze and improve stages of DMAIC. In these stages, interaction plots are useful for evaluating the results of designed experiments and multiple regression. Typically, plot variables are placed on the x-axis, and the responses are placed on the y-axis. The distinct lines on the plot are defined by the levels of the interaction variable. If the plot variables exhibit no interaction, then the lines basically will be parallel. That is, both plot variables will produce similar trends when combined with the response variable. If the lines are not parallel, however, an interaction likely exists.

EVOP strategy

Evolutionary operations (EVOP) most often are used during the analyze and improve stages of DMAIC. In the analyze stage, these strategies are used to assess the significance of various process factors. In the improve stage, these strategies are used to set new process factor specifications. One problem with evolutionary strategies is that they require a great many repetitions in order to isolate the effects of changes in factor levels. EVOP strategies usually take much longer than other designed experiments, and in some cases it may take months before the significance of process changes can be identified. However, productive operations may continue even while an evolutionary operations strategy is being implemented, which is not the case for designed experiments. Also, evolutionary operations strategies assess the process as currently performed, which means that any significant factors overlooked in a designed experiment automatically will become part of the system.

Creation
Evolutionary operations strategies assess performance on a cycle-by-cycle basis. For the purposes of EVOP, a cycle is defined as an interval in which data has been collected at each point in the process design. In evolutionary operations, several cycles are observed and then the experimental conditions are varied. Each set of cycles performed with the new operating conditions is called a phase. The difference between the edge points and the center point is called the change in the mean, or curvature. When implementing an evolutionary operations strategy, limiting adjustments to two or three factors is best. Otherwise, the experiment will be too complicated. The adjustments should be minor so their effects can be observed with precision. The best way to proceed with the experiment for two or three factors is to run it twice before estimating error and the effect significance. If the factor continues to be significant after three cycles, the next phase of the strategy should be performed with the conditions centered on the new optimal condition. If factors do not appear statistically significant, increasing the range of levels for these factors may be useful.

Redefining process flow

One way to improve processes is to redefine the process flows. A process may be simplified or optimized. Redundant steps may be removed, and level-loading techniques may be applied. Many businesses improve processes by reducing set-up times. Whenever process flows are redefined, assessing the impact on quality is important. The critical-to-quality metrics used during the measure stage are useful. Benchmarking is a common approach to redefining process flows. Benchmarking refers to a systematic review of similar or dissimilar processes in another organization. Too often, benchmarking is assumed a prelude to imitation. People incorrectly believe that benchmarking means mapping out a competitor's process and then copying it. Instead, businesses should use the information they obtain as inspiration.

Simulations

Many Six Sigma teams use simulations to inform their choices during the improve stage of DMAIC. A simulation is a cheap way to predict the likelihoods and effects of variable levels. Simulations can confirm the solutions derived from analysis and can indicate the possible interactions between variables. Simulations are useful for evaluating changing situations because the dynamics of the change can be built into the simulation. Simulations require a process model and a rough probability distribution for every variable. The simulation takes these distributions and creates a resulting frequency distribution. Simulations can be very informative, but they must be confirmed against hard data before or after they are run. Although simulations are not fool-proof method of research, they certainly are valuable relative to their cost.

Adjustment of operating conditions

During the improve stage, the Six Sigma team must identify or predict optimal operating conditions. This action can be difficult when many input factors contribute to performance. The overarching goal of adjusting operating conditions is to establish levels that provide satisfactory results with minimal variation. If the process model is complex, the best way to identify optimal operating conditions is with response surface techniques. These techniques narrow the regions in which optimal factor settings may occur. Another way to find the best operating conditions is with evolutionary operations, or EVOP. One advantage of EVOP is that it can be implemented as the process continues to run. Changes are made to the process in action instead of in an experimental condition.

Preventing deviation

Statistical process control
In Six Sigma, it is preferable almost always to prevent mistakes then to correct mistakes that already have occurred. Detection after the mistake is more expensive,

time-consuming, and difficult. Six Sigma teams find the inputs that lead to process variation. If the inputs are controlled, variations and errors can be minimized and even eliminated. Statistical process controls monitor the stability of input and output variables, although this process is more effective at monitoring inputs. If the process capability index C_{pk} is 1.5 or more, then a control chart may be used to assess the Six Sigma-level outputs are good enough. Statistical process control is one of the three common methods for controlling processes: the other two are engineering process control and operational procedures.

EPC

Engineering process control (EPC) is a mechanical system for automatically adjusting input in reponse to process variations. A refrigerator is equipped with a basic engineering process control: when the temperature inside rises too far from the desired level, a cooling engine lowers the temperature. The engineering process control devices used in industry are much more complicated. They can function with multiple inputs and outputs. When engineering process control devices are used, however, one cannot also use statistical process control charts, because the constant adjustment of the EPC system will influence the data. In other words, when engineering process control devices are used, the data collected from the process is not independent.

Operational procedures

Operational procedures are similar to engineering process control, except that humans, rather than machines, execute operational procedures. For this reason, operational procedures are subject to more errors. Still, in some cases, operational procedures still will be the best and cheapest option, especially in transactional processes. One common operational procedure is standardizing the process. For instance, the tellers at a bank could be taught to process deposits according to the same steps every time. Another operational procedure is separating orders by type. Many businesses streamline their responses to orders by dividing orders into several key categories. Another way to prevent deviation with operational procedures is establishing processes for diverting resources when needs are urgent. Operational procedures require careful observation and should be documented on process maps, flowcharts, or written summaries.

Standardizing new methods

The first task of the control stage is standardizing the new methods. The new protocols and processes should be in continuous improvement, but the advances made thus far should be written as policy. Too often, employees fall back into old and unproductive habits after the main thrust of the Six Sigma project is complete. One way to prevent this backsliding is to use process control to monitor process variation. One way to do this is to define the methods of control with a control plan. Another way involves writing out all process procedures and duties on process maps, flowcharts, and sets of work instructions. Process variation always should be monitored with process control. Finally, all employees should receive training in the new methods, and new employees should receive a comprehensive orientation.

Merits of process simplification

One of the most common strategies in Six Sigma involves simplifying needlessly complex processes. When the same process is used to create a wide variety of products and services, the process probably is too complicated. As much as possible, businesses should try to limit the variation in deliverables so processes can be standardized more effectively. When customers have more choices, cycle time tends to be longer. Another way to simplify processes involves restricting sales to a single type of customer. By focusing on a particular customer demographic, a business can preclude frequent requests for variation. One positive effect of reducing process complexity is that inventory levels can be diminished. If fewer modifications or customizations are performed during the creation of a product, fewer spare parts will be required as well.

Control charts to identify sources of variation

In the analyze stage of DMAIC, the Six Sigma team will look closely at the statistical control charts created during the measure stage. One of the initial goals of analysis will be to distinguish special and common causes of variation. Special causes of variation do not occur during every performance of the process, but when they do, they cause significant delay. On a control chart, special causes of variation will be indicated by points that lie far outside the normal range. The location of these out-of-control points will suggest possible sources of the variation. That is, it will be possible to see at which point during the process the variation occurred. Common causes of variation will influence each iteration of the process and therefore will not be obvious on a control chart. Several reasons for common cause variation may exist. Variations from common cause, then, may be more difficult to diagnose.

U charts

U charts are control charts designed to handle attributes data. A U chart depicts the percentage of samples that have a particular condition in situations where sample sizes may vary and each sample may have more than one occurrence of the condition. U charts are used during the measure and improve stages of DMAIC. In the measure stage, they use attributes data to estimate process baselines. In most cases, however, it is better to use a variable control chart for this purpose. In the improve stage, U charts occasionally are used to establish target figures, though the relative paucity of errors makes it difficult to use these chart so late in the project. In a U chart, the plotted statistic is $u_j = \frac{(\text{count})_j}{n_j}$, where n_j is the sample size of group j.

The centerline is $\bar{u} = \frac{\sum_{j=1}^{m}(\text{count})_j}{m}$, where m is the number of groups in the analysis.

The upper control limits are $\text{UCL} = \bar{u} + 3\sqrt{\dfrac{\bar{u}}{n_j}}$ and the lower control limits are

$\text{LCL} = \max\left(0, \bar{u} - 3\sqrt{\dfrac{\bar{u}}{n_j}}\right)$, where $\bar{u}$ is the average percent.

Interpretation

On a U chart, the upper and lower control limits indicate the boundaries of expected process behavior. The variation of points that lie within the control limits is attributed to common causes, while any points outside the statistical control must be attributed to special causes. If no special-cause variation exists, then the process is stable enough to be predictable. When special causes of variation exist, they must be identified and eliminated. The Six Sigma team will need to brainstorm possible sources of special-cause variation and then design experiments to test these hypotheses. In the meantime, it is possible to predict the behavior of the process once the special causes of variation have been removed. To make such a prediction, simply ignore all out-of-control points when calculating the average and the upper and lower control limits.

Statistical process control charts

Statistical process control charts use past performance to predict future variations. These charts can confirm the stability of a process. Statistical process control charts are used during the measure, analyze, improve, and control stages of DMAIC. In the measure stage, they convert common-cause variation into objective data that can be used to baseline processes. Also, statistical control charts can be used during the measure stage to evaluate the repeatability and reproducibility of a measurement system. In the analyze stage, statistical control charts can be used to distinguish common and special causes of variation. In the improve stage, statistical control charts can be used to confirm the success of process improvements. Finally, in the control stage of DMAIC, statistical control charts can be used to confirm the stability of adjusted processes and to confirm that the adjustments have improved the process.

Creation

All control charts hold certain characteristics in common. First, the x-axis value must be sequential on every chart. Often, time is plotted along the x-axis. The y-axis, on the other hand, will be for the statistic being charted for each unit on the x-axis. Also, a statistical process control chart will define limits for the plotted statistic. Control limits are calculated by observing process behavior. In order for a control chart to work, it must be derived from rational sub-groups (samples), or short-term variation will not indicate long-term variation. A sub-group is considered rational if the causes of within-subgroup variation are approximately the same as the causes of between-subgroup variation. In other words, any observed variation should be random. Each subgroup will indicate the current location in the process and the amount of variation at that location.

Required calculations for range and sigma charts

The plotted statistic for a range chart is calculated as follows: $\text{Range}_j = \max(x_1, x_2, \ldots, x_n) - \min(x_1, x_2, \ldots, x_n)$. The centerline is the average range. The upper control limits are calculated $\text{UCL}_R = \bar{R} + 3d_3\sigma_x$ and the lower control limits are calculated $\text{LCL}_R = \max(0, \bar{R} - 3d_3\sigma_x)$. In these equations, $\bar{R}$ is the average range, d_3 is a function of n, and σ_x is process sigma. In the calculation of process sigma, the average range is set as $\bar{R}/d_2$. In a sigma chart, the plotted statistic is the subgroup standard deviation, calculated $S_j = \sqrt{\frac{\sum_{i=1}^{n}(x_i - \bar{x}_j)^2}{n-1}}$, where x_i are the observations in subgroup j, $\bar{x}_j$ is the subgroup average for subgroup j, and n is the subgroup size. The centerline of the sigma chart is the average sigma. The upper control limits are calculated $\text{UCL}_S = \bar{S} + 3\left(\frac{\bar{S}}{c_4}\right)\sqrt{1 - c_4^2}$, and the lower control limits are calculated $\text{LCL}_S = \min\left[0, \bar{S} + 3(\bar{S}/c_4)\sqrt{1 - c_4^2}\right]$, where $\bar{S}$ is the average sigma and c_4 is a function of n.

P charts

P charts are a type of control chart primarily used for attributes data. A *P* chart measures the percentage of samples with a particular characteristic in situations where sample size may vary and the sample unit either will have the characteristic or not have the characteristic. *P* charts are used during the measure and improve stages of DMAIC. In the measure stage, they are effective at estimating the process baseline from the attributes data. However, using a variables control chart in this capacity generally is preferable. In the improve stage, *P* charts are used to estimate the number of errors. Like *Np* charts, however, they are not ideal for this purpose because of the low number of errors. *P* charts can be generated by Minitab, Excel, and other statistical software programs.

Creation
When creating a *P* chart, it is important to gather the samples from the same point in the process every time. Unlike an *Np* chart, in which the samples must have the same number of units, a *P* chart can be constructed from samples with varying numbers of units. For a *P* chart, the plotted statistic is the percentage of items in each sample that have the target characteristic. The plotted statistic is calculated $p_j = \frac{(\text{count})_j}{n_j}$, where n_j is the number of units taken from group j. The centerline is calculated with $\bar{p} = \frac{\sum_{j=1}^{m}(\text{count})_j}{\sum_{j=1}^{m} n_j}$. Again, n_j is the sample size of group j, and m is the number of groups included in analysis. The upper control limit is calculated with $\text{UCL} = \bar{p} + 3\sqrt{\frac{\bar{p}(1-\bar{p})}{n_j}}$, and the lower control limit with $\text{LCL} = \max\left[0, \bar{p} - 3\sqrt{\frac{\bar{p}(1-\bar{p})}{n_j}}\right]$. In both of these equations, $\bar{p}$ is the average percent.

Interpretation

On a *P* chart, all of the data points should lie between the upper and lower control limits. In such a case, the process is said to be in statistical control. As long as the data points remain within the control limits, any variation may be attributed to common causes. If all the data points are within the control limits, the process is said to be within statistical control and future performance can be predicted. However, if data points lie outside of the control limits, this must be blamed on special causes of variation. The next step for the Six Sigma team will be to consider possible sources of special-cause variation and then measure them with designed experiments. Even when a *P* chart contains some points outside the control limits, it is possible to predict the future process capability by simply removing the out-of-control points.

C charts

A C chart is a type of control chart appropriate for attributes data. A C chart tracks the number of events in a sample of a predetermined size. The distinguishing feature of a C chart is that the measured event may occur more than once in each unit of the sample. For instance, a C chart may be used to track errors in a particular process, with the knowledge that several errors might occur in a single iteration of the process. C charts typically are used during the measure and improve stages of DMAIC. During the measure stage, C charts are used to estimate process baselines with attributes data. IT may be better, however, to use a variables control chart for this purpose. In the improve stage, there may also be a role for the C chart, although hopefully by this point in the process the number of errors will be too small for the C chart to be the most effective.

Creation

Creating a C chart begins with selecting an appropriate sample. The samples must be taken from a specific part of the process at the same time. The important feature of the C chart is that each element of the sample may have more than one of the featured attributes. For instance, if the purpose of the C chart is to measure errors during a particular part of production, each instance of that process may contain more than one error. In a C chart, the plotted statistic is the number of occurrences of a particular event during the sample. The centerline of the chart is determined with the formula $\bar{c} = \frac{\sum_{j=1}^{m}(count)_j}{m}$, where m is the number of groups used in the analysis. The upper control limit of the chart is calculated UCL= $\bar{c} + 3\sqrt{\bar{c}}$, and the lower control limit is calculated LCL= $max(0, \bar{c} - 3\sqrt{\bar{c}})$. For both control limit formulae, $\bar{c}$ is the average count and n is the sample size.

X-bar charts

X-bar charts, sometimes called $\bar{X}$ charts, are control charts for variables data. These charts take the averages from subgroups (of observations) to get a view of the process location over time. X-bar charts are most useful during the measure, analyze, improve, and control stages of DMAIC. In the measure stage, they are used to baseline processes by identifying the inevitable amount of common-cause variation. They also are used in this stage to evaluate the repeatability and reproducibility of a measurement system. In the analyze stage, these charts are used to distinguish special and common causes of variation. In the improve stage, X-bar charts are used to confirm that implemented changes have improved the process metric. Finally, in the control stage, X-bar charts are used to ensure that processes remain statistically stable.

Implementation

X-bar charts are useful when subgroups of more than two observations can be measured. The x-axis of the X-bar chart is time, so the chart serves as a chronological model of the process, moving from left to right. Of course, all data entered into an X-bar chart must be assigned a time, or else special-cause variation may not be noticeable. If the size of the subgroup is greater than ten, then a range chart should not be used to monitor process variation, because it will do a poor job of estimating process sigma. Instead, a sigma chart should be used. If the subgroup sizes are 1, an exponentially weighted moving average or individual-X/moving-range chart may be used.

Required calculations

A certain set of calculations are required for an X-bar chart. These charts can be generated by Excel and Minitab. Before an X-bar chart can be created, the team must determine the appropriate subgroup size and sampling frequency. The plotted statistic for an X-bar chart is the subgroup average. The centerline is the grand average. The upper control limits are calculated $UCL_{\bar{x}} = \bar{\bar{x}} + 3\left(\frac{\sigma_x}{\sqrt{n}}\right)$, and the lower control limits are calculated $LCL_{\bar{x}} = \bar{\bar{x}} - 3\left(\frac{\sigma_x}{\sqrt{n}}\right)$. In these equations, $\bar{\bar{x}}$ is the grand average and σ_x is process sigma. Process sigma is calculated with either the subgroup range or the subgroup sigma statistic.

Interpretation

Before interpreting the X-bar chart, one must first examine the range chart. When the range chart is out of control, the control limits on the X-bar chart will not be useful. When the range chart contains points outside of statistical control, the special causes of this variation must be identified and eliminated. Some range charts will have only a few distinct values, suggesting that the chart needs better resolution. After any points outside statistical control have been removed, the X-bar chart may be interpreted relative to control limits and run-test rules. Any points on the X-bar chart outside statistical control must be eliminated. This elimination is accomplished in the usual way: the special causes of variation are identified through brainstorming and data analysis, and the operating conditions are adjusted accordingly.

EWMA charts

An exponentially weighted moving average (EWMA) chart is a type of control chart primarily used for variables data. The creator of the chart selects a weighting factor, which assigns different values to data depending on its age. This type of chart uses data from every available sample, so it can identify extremely small variations in the process. Exponentially weighted moving-average charts are used during the measure and control stages of DMAIC. In the measure stage, these charts are used to baseline a process. Exponentially weighted moving-average charts are valuable especially for this purpose when the process might be nonnormal and the rational subgroup size is only one. In the control stage, exponentially weighted moving-average charts are used to control the process, either for the reasons outlined in the measure stage or when it is necessary to detect extremely small shifts in the process. Given the same sample size, an exponentially weighted moving average chart can detect shifts from $1/2\sigma$ to 2σ faster than a Shewhart chart.

Creation

One of the most important initial steps in the creation of an exponentially weighted moving-average chart is setting the value for λ (lambda), the weighting factor. To detect small shifts, the value should be set around 0.2; to detect large shifts, the value should be set between 0.2 and 0.4. The plotted statistic for an EWMA is calculated with $z_t = \lambda_1 \bar{x}_t + (1 - \lambda_1)z_{t-1}$, where t is a particular time, λ is the value of the weighting factor, $\bar{x}_t$ is the subgroup average for the present subgroup at t, and the value of z at t_0 is either the overall average or a target. The control limits are calculated with $\text{CL}_{\text{EWMA}} = z_0 \pm \left(\frac{3\bar{R}}{d_2\sqrt{n}}\right)\sqrt{\frac{\lambda}{(2-\lambda)}[1 - (1 - \lambda)^{2t}]}$, where z_0 is the target value or process mean value, n is the size of the subgroup, m is the number of functions being analyzed, and d_2 is a function of n.

Interpretation

The first step in the interpretation of exponentially weighted moving-average charts is to examine the range chart. If this chart is out of statistical control, then the control limits found on the EWMA cannot be trusted. Any points out of statistical control should be linked to special causes of variation. The team may need to think creatively in order to discover the sources of process variation. After the range chart has been reviewed, the EWMA chart may be compared to the control limits. Run tests and specifications are irrelevant in the interpretation of EWMA charts, because process observations will display much broader variation. If the process appears to be stable, then it considering its capability relative to requirements may be useful.

Np charts

The *Np* chart is a control chart used to assess attributes data. This chart measures the number of times a condition exists in each sample, when the condition may occur only once and the sample size is consistent. *Np* charts are used during the measure and improve stages of DMAIC. In the measure stage, they use attributes data to guess the process baseline. Whenever possible, however, a variables control chart is used in lieu of an *Np* chart for this purpose. During the improve stage, *Np* charts are used to determine the number of errors in process samples. However, the relatively small number of errors in most processes makes the *Np* chart a somewhat ineffective tool for this purpose. *Np* charts can be generated on Excel, Minitab, and other statistical software programs.

<u>Creation</u>
To create an *Np* chart, it is necessary to gather sample data at the same point in each process. Also, every sample should have the same number of units. The plotted statistic is defined as the number of items in the sample that have the particular characteristic. The centerline of the chart is calculated with the following equation: $n\bar{p} = \frac{\sum_{j=1}^{m}(\text{count})_j}{m}$, in which m is the number of groups involved in the analysis. The upper control limits are calculated with the following formula: $\text{UCL}_{np} = n\bar{p} + 3\sqrt{n\bar{p}(1-\bar{p})}$. The lower control limits are calculated with the following formula: $\text{LCL}_{np} = \max[0, n\bar{p} - 3\sqrt{n\bar{p}(1-\bar{p})}]$. In each of the control limit calculations, the sample size is n and the average count is $n\bar{p}$. The value for $\bar{p}$ is calculated $\bar{p} = \frac{\sum_{j=1}^{m}(\text{count})_j}{m \times n}$.

<u>Interpretation</u>
An *Np* chart depicts a stable process when all of the data points lie between the upper and lower control limits. Any variation within these limits is due to common causes, but any variation that results in data points outside the control limits must be attributed to special causes. Data points that lie outside the control limits must be explained. Typically, an *Np* chart is succeeded by experimentation aimed at diagnosing particular causes. However, until these special causes of variation have been determined, the capability of the process can be predicted by eliminating the data points that lie outside the control. This elimination will remove the extreme data points from the formulae for average and control limits, which will provide a more reasonable estimate of future performance.

Individual-X and moving-range charts

Individual-X and moving-range charts are control charts used to assess variables data. A moving-range chart depicts changes in variation between consecutive subgroups over an interval. An individual-X chart assesses the process location over an interval using a subgroup with a single observation. Individual-X and moving-range charts are used during the measure, analyze, improve, and control stages of DMAIC. In the measure stage, these charts are used to baseline processes by creating an objective measure of inherent process variations. In the analyze stage, these charts are used to distinguish special and common causes for variation. In the improve stage, these charts are used to confirm the results of improvements. Finally, in the control stage, these charts are used to confirm the stability of improved processes.

Creation of individual-X charts

In an individual-X chart, the plotted statistic is the observation. For a normal distribution, the centerline is the average. For a non-normal distribution, the centerline is the median of the fitted distribution. The upper control limit is calculated $UCL_x = \bar{x} + 3\sigma_x$ and the lower control limit is calculated $LCL_x = \bar{x} - 3\sigma_x$, where σ_x is the process sigma and $\bar{x}$ is the average. When the process is non-normal, the upper control limit is set at the 99.865 percentile of the fitted curve, and the lower control limit is set at the 0.135 percentile. Selecting a distribution curve can be difficult because the control limits are based on the curve, but the curve cannot be set until it is verified that the process is under statistical control. For this reason, many people prefer to use the EWMA or some other chart to establish process control so a distribution can be assigned to the data.

Creation of moving-range charts

In a moving-range chart, the plotted statistic is the moving range, or the difference between the immediate observation and the immediately preceding observation of the sub-groups in an individual-X chart. The moving range is calculated $MR = |x_j - x_{j-1}|$. The centerline is calculated $\overline{MR} = \frac{1}{m-1}\sum_{j-1}^{m} MR_j$, where m is the total number of subgroups and MR_j is the moving range for subgroup j. The upper control limit is calculated $UCL_{MR} = \overline{MR} + 3d_3\sigma_x$ and the lower control limit is calculated as $LCL_{MR} = \max(0, \overline{MR} - 3d_3\sigma_x)$, in which $\overline{MR}$ is the average of the moving ranges, d_3 is a function of n, and σ_x is the process sigma. If a process has a normal distribution, then the moving-range chart will not display any special causes not also displayed on the individual-X chart.

Interpretation

After an individual-X chart is completed, it should be searched for special-cause variation. Any special causes of variation must be identified and removed. During this identification and removal, the future capability of the process can be predicted by eliminating any out-of-control points from the analysis. Special causes of variation should be identified and studied in designed experiments. The general strategy when interpreting individual-X and moving-range charts is to find non-random behavior or trends in the data. One way to find these trends is to apply the run-test rules. Once a process has been observed for a sufficient time and is found to be in control, calculating the process capability relative to requirements is possible. However, it is not possible to predict the capability of a process not in statistical control.

Run-test

Rules

Western Electric created run-test rules as additions to the standard control chart. The purpose of these tests is to identify patterns in the plotted points on a control chart. There are eight run tests in all. All eight of the tests can be used for $\bar{X}$ and individual-X charts. The first four run tests can be used for P, U, Np, and C charts. In run test 1, there is one subgroup with more than three standard deviations from the mean, which suggests a shift in the process mean. Run test 2 has nine consecutive subgroups on one side of the average. In run test 3, six subgroups in a row either increase or decrease. In run test 4, fourteen consecutive subgroups alternate being greater or smaller than the preceding and succeeding subgroups. In run test 5, two of the three consecutive subgroups are greater than two standard deviations from the mean. In run test 6, four out of five subgroups in a row are greater than one standard deviation from the mean. In run test 7, fifteen consecutive subgroups are within one standard deviation. Finally, in run test 8, eight points in a row are more than one standard deviation from the center.

Typical application

On m and individual-X charts where the normal distribution is used, run tests are applied as they were written in the Western Electric Statistical Quality Control Handbook. On an individual-X chart for which a non-normal distribution has been used, the median is substituted for the average. Also, on these charts, it is necessary to establish zones that produce the same probabilities as the normal curve for the given standard deviation. When applying run tests to the upper and lower halves of a control chart, run tests 1, 2, 5, and 6 should be applied separately. The other run tests (3, 4, 7, and 8) are applied to the entire chart. The option to use run tests is typical of statistical process control programs.

Interpretation

Run tests either identify shifts in the process mean (1, 2, 3, 5, and 6) or provide information about sampling errors (4, 7, and 8). Run test 4 suggests that samples have been taken from a multi-stream process, while run test 7 suggests that sample stratification exists. Run test 8 suggests that samples have been taken from a mixture. Very occasionally, run charts incorrectly may identify errors in the statistical control chart. For the most part, however, these tests are effective at identifying problems in data collection. It should be noted that run tests alert the user to errors but are not as effective at locating those errors. For many of these tests, a good number of data points must pass through before the run test is activated. Therefore, when a run test is violated the user should go back and analyze the data to discover its location.

Training

Even when a Six Sigma project is accompanied by massive documentation and comprehensive control plans, employee training is very important for maintaining improvements. Employees should learn the updated processes, of course, but they also should learn the most important process factors and inputs. Sometimes this information will not seem necessary strictly for the performance of the employee's job, but a little context gives the employee a sense of the rationale for changes. Training shows the employee why the process changes will improve his or her work. Training sessions should include employees from different departments and levels of the organization. However, it training sessions should be pitched to the level of the audience so all employees will understand the content. All training sessions should conclude with some sort of evaluation in order to gauge employee comprehension.

Implementation and verification of changes

For many Six Sigma professionals, the implementation of changes during the improve stage of DMAIC is the most exciting part of a project. At this point, the solutions crafted by the team finally are realized. Communication and documentation must be constant at this point so any problems can be identified and resolved. It may be useful to receive explicit authority from the sponsor before making changes so other employees recognize the importance of buy-in. In any case, participating employees should be given comprehensive instructions and should be monitored closely during the initial phases of implementation. In the best case scenario, the first results will verify the wisdom of the solution and will generate sufficient data for statistical analysis. Once the process can be confirmed as stable and acceptable, it can be enshrined as the new method of operation.

Documentation at the close of the control stage

The final results of the Six Sigma project will be summarized in a project report. This report should begin with the project charter. The report also should include a summary of the results from each DMAIC stage. The report should provide objective indications of whether the short- and long-term goals were met. These objective conclusions should be buttressed with raw data and analysis, which may be included in an appendix to the report. The project report should outline the expenditures and the cost savings related to the project and should outline the control plan designed to keep the project's changes in place. Finally, the project report should include some recommendations or suggestions for future projects in this line.

Control plans

A control plan is a general summary of the detection and/or prevention strategies used to control processes or materials. Control plans most often are used during the control stage of DMAIC. They are used to create a record of the strategy used to control the key process variables. A control plan generally is compiled from the results of designed experiments and failure modes and effects analysis. This latter analysis is important because it indicates the most important sources of failure to control. The characteristics that need to be monitored and controlled will be listed along the left side of the control chart. For each characteristic, there will be a specification, measurement technique, sample size, sample frequency, analytical tool, and reaction protocol.

Basic components

Control plans list all of the information related to error prevention and detection efforts. This information is based on designed experiments and failure modes and effects analysis. These processes indicate the processes and inputs that need to be monitored and controlled. The risk priority number generated during FMEA designates the most important failure modes in a process. A comprehensive control plan includes basic information such as the specification related to each relevant characteristic. On a control chart, the specification is the objective range within which the characteristic tolerably can fall. The control chart also should indicate how the characteristic will be measured and how many measurements will be included in each sample. A control chart also should indicate how often samples will be obtained and the analytical tool with which they will be evaluated. Finally, a complete control chart will include the reaction rules, the response protocols when the characteristic does not meet the specifications.

Listed information

A control plan typically provides six pieces of information for every characteristic: specification, measurement technique, sample size, sample frequency, analytical tool, and reaction protocol. The specification defines what is considered acceptable and unacceptable for this characteristic. It should be expressed as an objective value. For instance, the specification for an oven might be 400 degrees if it needs to be at this temperature in order to function properly. The measurement technique is the equipment and protocol for assessing the specifications. The sample size is the number of measurements required at every collection time. The sample frequency indicates the interval between each successive data collection. The analytical tool is the system for analyzing the measurements. For instance, some characteristics will be monitored with control charts, so any adverse trends can be detected. Finally, the reaction protocols on a control plan will be the directions for employees in the event that a characteristic requires adjustment.

Level loading

Level loading is one of the more common lean tools. Its purpose is to regulate and moderate the flow of orders in a particular process. Level loading typically is performed during the improve stage of DMAIC. Specifically, this tool can be useful for diminishing the need for inventory checks during a process. Before level loading can be implemented, protocols must be standardized and employees must be trained in multiple areas. The first step in level loading is to calculate the takt time, or the target process time. This calculation should equal the demand divided by the amount of time available. Takt time should be posted at the work station, and resources should be aligned with it. When variations in demand exist, needs for increased resources also will exist. The intention of level loading strategies is to eliminate wait time at the beginning of processes. Each completed unit should begin the next phase of the production process immediately. There should be a protocol in place for adjusting resources to meet the natural fluctuations in demand.

5S

5S is a lean tool whose name is derived from a set of Japanese words related to organizational hygiene: organization, purity, cleanliness, discipline, and tidiness. For the purposes of American audiences, these words are sometimes translated as sort, straighten, shine, standardize, and sustain. 5S is used most often during the improve stage of DMAIC. Here, it is a valuable strategy for reducing cycle time that does not add value and that is lost to movement, finding lost materials, and inefficiently using the physical space. 5S may also be used to accelerate inventory processes and to diminish accidents in the workplace. The program is implemented according to a five-level system. At the first level, the organization has not been subjected to lean management processes. By the time the fifth level is reached, maximum efficiency and minimum waste have been achieved. In Six Sigma, the data collected according to such a rating system often is placed on a radar chart, which indicates the strengths and weaknesses of each department.

Efforts to prevent human error

A Six Sigma team will work to minimize the chances and significance of human error in processes. The typical approach involves dividing human error into three categories: willful, technique, and inadvertent. Willful errors are made on purpose by disgruntled employees. For obvious reasons, they can be difficult to predict and stop. The best way to diminish willful errors is to keep employees happy. Technique errors occur because employees are poorly trained or don't understand processes. Technique errors are not made on purpose, and sometimes they are committed without the employee's awareness. In most cases, technique errors are limited to a particular task or employee. Inadvertent errors are the normal variations that occur in any human endeavor. An inadvertent error happens rarely but cannot be eliminated entirely as long as a person is performing the task. Automating the process is one way to eliminate these errors. Another way to minimize inadvertent errors is to conform the workspace to the physical dimensions of the person so movements are more natural.

Practice Test

Practice Questions

1. In businesses that apply the theory of constraints, which element of a process receives immediate attention?
    a. The most problematic
    b. The most important
    c. The most efficient
    d. The most complicated

2. What is one major problem with obtaining information about customer satisfaction from comment cards?
    a. Participants must be compensated.
    b. The most pleased and displeased customers are overrepresented.
    c. Responses are often vague.
    d. The expense is high.

3. Which distribution is appropriate for a continuous set of data with a fixed lower boundary but no upper boundary?
    a. Johnson
    b. exponential
    c. normal
    d. Logormal

4. What are the three most important characteristics of process metrics?
    a. Rationality, reliability, and repeatability
    b. Reliability, reproducibility, and repeatability
    c. Reliability, responsibility, and rationality
    d. Repeatability, responsibility, and reproducibility

5. Which pioneer of quality control wrote *Quality Is Free*?
    a. W. Edward Deming
    b. Joseph M. Juran
    c. Armand V. Feigenbaum
    d. Philip B. Crosby

6. Which of the following conflict-response strategies would be most appropriate when a group is fragile?
    a. Collaboration
    b. Competition
    c. Avoidance
    d. Accommodation

7. Which is typically the first category to be identified in SIPOC analysis?
   a. Suppliers
   b. Inputs
   c. Outputs
   d. Processes

8. How is takt time calculated?
   a. Available time divided by demand
   b. Overall process time minus time required for a particular task
   c. Demand divided by the amount of time available
   d. Time required for a task divided by demand

9. How many runs would be required in a complete factorial design if there are four levels and three factors?
   a. 7
   b. 12
   c. 64
   d. 81

10. Which parameter of a statistical distribution relates to the sharpness of its peak?
   a. Central tendency
   b. Kurtosis
   c. Skewness
   d. Standard deviation

11. What is the name for the amount of completed product divided by the original amount of product?
   a. Scrap rate
   b. Throughput yield
   c. Yield
   d. Rolled throughput yield

12. Which method of creating a prioritization matrix is appropriate when time is limited?
   a. Partial analytical method
   b. Consensus-criteria method
   c. Full analytical method
   d. Summary method

13. In gauge repeatability and reproducibility analysis, what percentage of total process variation is acceptable?
   a. 10% or less
   b. 15% or less
   c. 20% or less
   d. 30% or less

14. Which type of diagram is used to eliminate unnecessary movement during a process?
    a. Spaghetti diagram
    b. Scatter diagram
    c. Ishikawa diagram
    d. Matrix diagram

15. In what order are the process steps presented in a process decision program chart?
    a. Right to left
    b. Left to right
    c. Top to bottom
    d. Bottom to top

16. During which phase of response surface analysis is the direction of maximum response identified using the steepest ascent methodology?
    a. Phase 0
    b. Phase 1
    c. Phase 2
    d. Phase 3

17. In which method of sampling is a population divided into groups and a sample taken from each group?
    a. Systematic sampling
    b. Stratified sampling
    c. Judgment sampling
    d. Cluster sampling

18. In an analysis of variance, how is the F statistic used?
    a. To compare the mean square treatment with the mean square error
    b. To estimate the process average
    c. To find the variation within each subgroup
    d. To find the variation between different subgroups

19. Which of the following characteristics of a team most often results in groupthink?
    a. Frequent communication
    b. Lack of accountability
    c. Lack of subject expertise
    d. Undefined roles

20. In response surface analysis, which of the following values for s and t weights would indicate that the upper and lower boundaries are more important than the target?
    a. -0.3
    b. 0
    c. 1
    d. .7

21. Which of the following would be considered a value-added activity?
    a. Design
    b. Delivery
    c. Marketing
    d. Manufacturing

22. Which type of human error is typically limited to a particular task?
    a. Willful
    b. Inadvertent
    c. Technique
    d. Selective

23. Which of the following is a disadvantage of using engineering process control devices to prevent deviation?
    a. The devices must be monitored by human operators.
    b. The use of these devices precludes the use of statistical process controls.
    c. These devices require constant maintenance.
    d. These devices cannot handle multiple inputs.

24. Which type of chart is appropriate when sample size is variable and each sample may contain more than one instance of the targeted condition?
    a. P chart
    b. Autocorrelation chart
    c. U chart
    d. X-bar chart

25. From whose perspective is value defined in the lean methodology?
    a. Customer
    b. Chief executive
    c. Entry-level employee
    d. Competitor

26. On an X-bar chart, what variable is always represented on the x-axis?
    a. Variations
    b. Errors
    c. Length
    d. Time

27. Which of the following diagrams indicates the critical path of a process?
    a. Gantt chart
    b. Work breakdown structure
    c. Value stream analysis
    d. Matrix diagram

28. Which of the following is a disadvantage of higher-order multiple regression models?
    a. These models do a poor job of defining the area around a stationary point.
    b. Comprehensive and detailed experiments must be performed on the main effects.
    c. These models rarely have clear peaks and valleys.
    d. Small regions are difficult to perceive.

29. If there are 32 observations in an experiment, it is typical to run autocorrelations from lag 1 to:
    a. Lag 4
    b. Lag 8
    c. Lag 16
    d. Lag 32

30. During which stage of DMAIC is it most useful to calculate process velocity?
    a. Analyze
    b. Define
    c. Control
    d. Improve

31. In kaizen, the idea that one step in a process should be completed only when the subsequent steps are ready is referred to as:
    a. Flow
    b. Poka-yoke
    c. Pull
    d. Perfection

32. Which type of Pareto chart would be the least useful?
    a. One in which the bars represent costs
    b. One in which the cumulative percentage line is steep
    c. One in which all the bars are roughly the same height
    d. One in which the bars on the left are significantly taller than the bars on the right

33. If all of the data points on an *Np* chart fall between the upper and lower control limits, the process is:
    a. Representative
    b. Stable
    c. Efficient
    d. Erratic

34. According to Little's law, the number of items included in a process divided by the number of process completions per hour is the:
    a. Process lead time
    b. Value-added time
    c. Velocity
    d. Process cycle efficiency

35. In nominal group technique, how many pieces of paper should each participant receive if there are 40 options to be considered?
    a. 2
    b. 4
    c. 6
    d. 8

36. When a batch sample has upper and lower specifications, which statistic is used in the creation of a process performance index?
    a. P_p
    b. P_{pk}
    c. P_{pl}
    d. C_p

37. Which of the following factors is not included in the calculation of risk priority number?
    a. Detection level
    b. Severity
    c. Expense
    d. Likelihood

38. Which of the following run tests identifies shifts in the process mean?
    a. Run test 4
    b. Run test 6
    c. Run test 7
    d. Run test 8

39. Which of the following autocorrelation functions would indicate the strongest correlation?
    a. 0.1
    b. -0.8
    c. 0.9
    d. -0.2

40. Which distribution should be used when the targeted characteristic may appear more than once per unit?
    a. Binomial
    b. Exponential
    c. Lognormal
    d. Poisson

41. Which Six Sigma methodology is more appropriate for existing processes?
    a. DMADV
    b. IDOV
    c. DMAIC
    d. DFSS

42. Which of the following distributions would be appropriate for discrete data?
    a. Exponential
    b. Poisson
    c. Normal
    d. Johnson

43. Which goodness-of-fit test focuses on the relationship between number of data points and distributional fit?
    a. Nonparametric test
    b. Kolmogorov-Smirnov test
    c. Chi-square test
    d. Anderson-Darling test

44. In hypothesis testing, why is it better to set a p value than to select a significance level?
    a. It ensures that a true hypothesis will not be rejected.
    b. It is then easier to make adjustments later in the experiment.
    c. It enables the collection of more samples.
    d. It makes it possible to reject the null hypothesis.

45. How are decisions represented in the ANSI set of flowchart symbols?
    a. Circles
    b. Squares
    c. Rectangles
    d. Diamonds

46. During which stage of DMAIC is the 5S method used most often?
    a. Define
    b. Measure
    c. Analyze
    d. Improve

47. In a histogram, the number of bars is equal to:
    a. The square root of the total number of data values
    b. The square root of the range of data
    c. The range of data divided by the total number of data values
    d. The number of data observations

48. Which statistical distribution is appropriate for continuous data with neither an upper nor a lower boundary?
    a. Lognormal
    b. Weibull
    c. Exponential
    d. Normal

49. In a contour plot, what is indicated by a series of evenly spaced parallel lines?
    a. First-order main effects
    b. Second-order main effects
    c. Interactions between two responses
    d. Interactions between three responses

50. Which of the following increases the power of an estimation of the confidence interval on the mean?
    a. A sample population with a normal distribution
    b. A smaller number of samples
    c. A known standard deviation
    d. An unknown standard deviation

Answers and Explanations

1. A: The most problematic. In businesses that apply the theory of constraints, the most problematic element of a process receives immediate attention. Indeed, the most problematic area is known as the constraint. The focus of improvement will be reducing the constraint without diminishing performance in any other area of the process. Once the targeted constraint has been diminished so that is no longer the most problematic component of the process, another area of the process will be addressed.

2. B: The most pleased and displeased customers are overrepresented. One major problem with obtaining information about customer satisfaction from comment cards is that the most pleased and displeased customers are overrepresented. That is, customers who have extreme opinions, whether positive or negative, will be the most motivated to comment. Businesses that use comment cards may find them to be a valuable source of specific information, but should avoid assuming that commenters are representative of the larger body of customers. Some of the advantages of comment cards are that they are relatively inexpensive and tend to elicit detailed feedback. Also, participation by customers is voluntary and does not require compensation.

3. D: Lognormal. A lognormal distribution is appropriate for a continuous set of data with a fixed lower boundary but no upper boundary. In most cases, the lower boundary on a lognormal distribution is zero. These distributions can be tested with a goodness-of-fit test. A Johnson distribution is more appropriate for continuous data that for whatever reason is inappropriate for a normal or exponential distribution. An exponential distribution is appropriate for any set of continuous data, though these distributions are most often used for frequency data. A normal distribution is appropriate for a set of continuous data with neither an upper nor a lower boundary. The normal distribution follows the pattern of the classic bell curve.

4. B: Reliability, reproducibility, and repeatability. The three most important characteristics of process metrics are reliability, reproducibility, and repeatability. Reliability is the extent to which the results of an experiment can be trusted to represent accurately the process being measured. Reproducibility is the extent to which a metric can be applied in different situations and obtain a reliable result. Repeatability is the extent to which a metric can be applied to the same situation multiple times and achieve the same result.

5. D: Philip B. Crosby. Philip B. Crosby wrote *Quality is Free*, a book that revolutionized quality management by placing an explicit emphasis on getting processes right the first time. Crosby insisted that businesses are better served by

investing more money in quality control on the first run, and thereby avoiding the costs of defective products. W. Edwards Deming is famous for enumerating the seven deadly diseases of the workplace and fourteen points of emphasis for management. Joseph M. Juran stressed the importance of customer satisfaction as a goal of quality control. Armand V. Feigenbaum is known for emphasizing four key actions in the implementation of quality management: establishing standards; creating metrics for conformance to these standards; resolving issues that impede conformance; and planning for continuous improvement.

6. D: Accommodation. When a group is fragile, the most appropriate conflict response strategy would be accommodation. Accommodation is the temporary sacrifice of personal desires in the name of group consensus. If a group is in danger of falling apart, the best way to handle a conflict may be to temporarily put aside differences in order to make progress in other areas. Collaboration or competition may be too risky for a fragile group, and avoidance of the conflict only jeopardizes the long-term health of the group by failing to resolve the underlying issues.

7. C: Outputs. In SIPOC analysis, the first category to be identified is outputs. SIPOC (suppliers, inputs, processes, outputs, and customers) analysis is typically performed during the define stage of DMAIC. Its intention is to identify the most important processes and the relevant stakeholders. At the beginning of SIPOC analysis, it is typical to create a process map or flowchart. Outputs are the first category to be identified, because the identification of outputs facilitates the identification of suppliers, inputs, and customers.

8. C: Demand divided by the amount of time available. Takt time is calculated by dividing demand by the amount of time available. This value, which is also known as target process time, should be posted at each workstation during the process of level loading. The takt time is the maximum amount of time a process can take without slowing down the overall completion of the task.

9. C: 64. If there are four levels and three factors in a complete factorial design, 64 runs would be required. The number of required runs is calculated by raising the number of levels to a power equal to the number of factors. In this case, then, the calculation is performed $4^3 = 64$. If the complete factorial design had five levels and three factors, the number of runs would be calculated $5^3 = 125$.

10. B: Kurtosis. Kurtosis is the parameter of a statistical distribution related to the sharpness of the peak. In a normal distribution, where the points resemble the standard bell curve, the kurtosis value is one. If the peak is sharper, the kurtosis value will be higher than one; if the peak is less severe; the kurtosis value will be less than one. Central tendency is the general trend of the data: in an asymmetrical distribution, the median is roughly equivalent to the central tendency, while in an asymmetrical distribution, the mean is a better marker. Skewness is basically the difference between the mean and the mode of a data set. The mode of the data set is

the value that appears most often. Finally, the standard deviation of the data set is the average amount of variation from the mean.

11. C: Yield. Yield is the amount of completed product divided by the original amount of product. This is one of the more popular critical-to-quality metrics. The ideal yield is one (or 100%). Scrap rate, meanwhile, is the percentage of materials not ultimately used in products. Throughput yield is the average percentage of completed units with no defects. Rolled throughput yield, finally, is the quality level that can be anticipated after several steps in the process have been completed.

12. B: Consensus-criteria method. When time is limited, the consensus-criteria method should be used to create a prioritization matrix. In this method, a group of people is each allotted a hundred points, which they then allocate across a series of criteria according to perceived importance. Prioritization matrices are used to identify those projects that will create the most value improvement over the long term. Also, organizations use participation matrices to identify the projects that will contribute the most to the achievement of the organizational goals. Besides the consensus-criteria method, the other method for creating a prioritization matrix is called the full analytical method. In this method, all of the various options are listed, and the members of the team assign a numerical value to each.

13. A: 10% or less. In gauge repeatability and reproducibility analysis, 10% or less total process variation is acceptable. Variation from 10 to 30% is considered problematic, and any variation over 30% is unacceptable. A gauge repeatability and reproducibility analysis may result in a statistic expressed as a percentage of total process variation or a percentage of tolerance. The range of acceptable percentages is the same when the statistic generated is a percentage of tolerance. Gauge repeatability and reproducibility analysis indicates the degree to which a measurement system avoids common- and special-cause variation.

14. A: Spaghetti diagram. A spaghetti diagram indicates the physical travel of employees, resources, and equipment during a process. These diagrams are used to identify unnecessary movements and to streamline processes as much as possible. A scatter diagram displays the correlation between two variables, with the independent variable on the *x*-axis and the dependent variable on the *y*-axis. An Ishikawa diagram, also known as a fishbone or cause-and-effect diagram, is used to outline the causes of a particular event, as well as the possible results of particular actions. Finally, a matrix diagram depicts the relationships between a group of different items in several groups. A matrix diagram looks a great deal like a table of data, with the strength between relationships indicated by the values in each cell.

15. A: Right to left. In a process decision program chart, the process steps are presented from right to left. A process decision program chart is used to isolate possible problems with a particular process or strategy. These charts are typically used during the Analyze and Improve stages of DMAIC. At the top of the chart, the process is named. The steps in the process are then presented from right to left,

with any necessary substeps mentioned underneath. Then the potential problems in each step are listed, along with some brainstormed solutions.

16. B: Phase 1. During Phase 1 of response surface analysis, the direction of maximum response is identified with the steepest ascent methodology. This methodology is also used to define the current operating region. Phase 0 involves the use of screening designs to assemble a basic list of significant factors and create a first-order regression model. Phase 2 is the application of ridge analysis and a second-order model. The intention of Phase 2 of response surface analysis is to identify optimal conditions at the stationary points in a limited region. There is no Phase 3 in response surface analysis.

17. B: Stratified sampling. In stratified sampling, the population is divided into groups, and a sample is taken from each group. In systematic sampling, on the other hand, there is a particular order to the selection of samples. In judgment sampling, an expert or group of experts selects the samples. In cluster sampling, experts create a representative group from which a random sample is drawn.

18. A: To compare the mean square treatment with the mean square error. In an analysis of variance, the F statistic is used to compare the mean square treatment with the mean square error. The mean square treatment is the average variation between the subsets, while the mean square error is the sum of the squares of the residuals. In order to trust the results of the F statistic, one must assume that the subsets have a normal distribution and unequal variance. The variation within each subgroup is calculated by taking repeated samples from the subgroup. The variation between different subgroups is found by comparing the averages of each subgroup.

19. C: Lack of subject expertise. When a team has a lack of subject expertise, it is more likely to suffer from groupthink. Groupthink is a phenomenon in which team members agree too readily, without adequately challenging each other's ideas. When groupthink occurs, a team will often select the first proposed solution to a problem, even if it has serious weaknesses. Groupthink is more likely to be a problem when the team members do not have enough experience or expertise in the subject area to come up with alternatives to a recommendation. Also, if the team members do not feel empowered to offer their views, they may be more likely to engage in groupthink.

20. D: 7. In response surface analysis, values of .7 for the s and t weights would indicate that the upper and lower boundaries are more important than the target. In Phase 2 of response surface analysis, the s and t weights are based on the relationship between the target and the boundary. When the target and the boundary have equal value, the s and t weights are 1. When the target is more important than the boundary, the s and t weights are between 1 and 10. When the boundary is more important than the target, the s and t weights are between 0.1 and 1.

21. D: Manufacturing. Manufacturing is considered a value-added activity. Value-added activities are those that create value in a product or service from the perspective of the customer. There are certain processes that are necessary but that do not add value for the customer. These are known as business-value-added activities. Design, delivery, and marketing are classic examples of business-value-added activities, because they do not directly add value for the customer, but they are a necessary part of the production process.

22. C: Technique. Technique error is typically limited to a particular task. Six Sigma experts identify three categories of human error: technique, inadvertent, and willful. Technique errors are the result of a lack of comprehension or poor training. It is more likely that technique errors will occur on difficult tasks. Inadvertent errors are slightly different, because they occur by accident even when an employee is experienced and understands the task. It is impossible to eliminate entirely inadvertent errors so long as there are human operators. A willful error is made intentionally by an employee. The best way to reduce willful errors is to maintain high morale and incentivize high performance.

23. B: The use of these devices precludes the use of statistical process controls. One disadvantage of using engineering process controls to prevent deviation is that the use of these devices precludes the use of statistical process controls. An engineering process control is a mechanism that automatically adjusts inputs when it detects variations in the process. A thermostat is a basic example of an engineering process control. It is not necessary for these devices to be monitored by human operators, and in most cases engineering process controls do not require constant maintenance. The constant adjustments made by these devices, however, mean that any data related to their activities is not independent, and therefore cannot be analyzed with statistical process control charts. However, the engineering process controls used by heavy industry are capable of handling a number of different inputs and outputs simultaneously.

24. C: U chart. A U chart is appropriate when sample size is variable and each sample may contain more than one instance of the targeted condition. These are control charts most appropriate for handling attributes data. A P chart, on the other hand, is better for measuring the percentage of samples with a particular characteristic when sample size is variable and the characteristic will either be present or absent. An autocorrelation chart indicates the relationships between various factors in the process. An X-bar chart, finally, is a control chart for variables data, in which the subgroup averages are assessed to determine the process location variation over time.

25. A: Customer. In the lean methodology, value is always defined from the perspective of the customer. This was a radical shift in perspective when it was first introduced. Most businesses assessed value from the perspective of executives or in-house experts. In lean methodology, value is defined as the qualities or characteristics for which a customer is willing to compensate the business.

26. D: Time. On an X-bar chart, time is always represented on the *x*-axis. X-bar charts are control charts for variables data. The chart should resemble a chronological model of the process: as the bars move away from the *y*-axis, they represent the advancement of time. In order for an X-bar chart to be possible, any variation must be assigned a time value. Outlying values on the X-bar chart indicate the presence of special-cause variation.

27. A: Gantt chart. A Gantt chart indicates the critical path of a process. The critical path is the sequence of steps that have a direct bearing on the overall length of the process. Some steps can be delayed without elongating the overall duration of the process: these steps are not considered to be on the critical path. A work breakdown structure depicts the organization of a process. To create a work breakdown structure, one isolates the various components of a problem and then considers the various contingencies associated with each component. A value stream analysis determines the elements of a process that add value to the finished product. These elements are targeted for special attention. Finally, a matrix diagram depicts the relative strengths of the relationships between the items in different groups. A matrix diagram might indicate causal relationships between various factors in a process or might simply indicate which of the factors are related.

28. B: Comprehensive and detailed experiments must be performed on the main effects. One disadvantage of higher-order multiple regression models is that comprehensive and detailed experiments must be performed on the main effects. Otherwise, it will not be wise to assume that the results of the higher-order multiple regression models are useful or accurate. However, higher-order multiple regression models have a number of advantages. For one thing, they are excellent at clearly defining the area around a stationary point. They typically have well-defined peaks and valleys, which facilitates analysis. Also, they are very effective at mapping small regions in the process, so they are able to achieve a high level of precision and detail.

29. B: Lag 8. If there are 32 observations in an experiment, it is typical to run autocorrelations from lag 1 to lag 8. The basic calculation for the number of autocorrelations in an experiment is lag 1 to lag $x/4$, in which x is the number of observations. Since there are 32 observations in this experiment, autocorrelations should run from lag 1 to lag 8. The lag is the difference between correlated observations. In lag 1, for instance, observation 1 is correlated with observation 2, observation 2 is correlated with observation 3, and observation 3 is correlated with observation 4, and so on. In lag 8, observation 1 would be correlated with observation 9, observation 2 with observation 10, observation 3 with observation 11, and so on. An experiment with 32 observations would include all of the intervening correlations between lag 1 and lag 8 (that is, lags 2 through 7).

30. A: Analyze. It is most useful to calculate process velocity during the analyze stage of DMAIC. Process velocity is the rate at which a particular phase of the process adds

value. Obviously, the higher the process velocity, the better. This metric is most useful during the analyze stage of DMAIC because it can be used to prioritize methods for improving cycle time. Velocity is typically calculated by dividing the number of value-added steps by the process lead time, which is the number of items in the process divided by the number of process completions per hour. Of course, as with any metric of quality, process velocity is somewhat subjective.

31. C: Pull. In kaizen, the idea that one step in a process should be completed only when the subsequent steps are ready is referred to as pull. This is opposite to the typical arrangement in manufacturing processes, in which materials are pushed through the process chain as they are completed. Kaizen recommends instead that materials be drawn along by vacuums created in the production chain. A process chain in which this occurs is said to have pull. Flow, meanwhile, is the continuous completion of a process. Organizations that adopt the kaizen philosophy attempt to make flow constant in every department and stage of processes. Poka-yoke is a Japanese system for error-proofing, based on the premise that avoiding errors in the first run is worth a slightly higher cost. Perfection is the kaizen ideal of continuous improvement. Perfection is a goal that can never be attained but should be strived towards regardless.

32. C: One in which all the bars are roughly the same height. The least useful type of Pareto chart would be one in which all the bars are roughly the same height. A Pareto chart is used to identify the most important and urgent problems in a process. It is based on the Pareto principle, which is basically that a process can be improved dramatically through attention to the few most important problems. It is essential that the bars on a Pareto chart represent fungible values, like cost or count. A Pareto chart will not be useful if it is based on percentages or rates. The most useful Pareto charts have several large bars on the left, indicating problems that are significantly more important than others. Similarly, a steeply ascending line on a Pareto chart indicates that a few of the identified factors are very important, and therefore that the chart will be useful. If all of the bars on a Pareto chart are roughly the same height, no one factor is more important than another, meaning it will be impossible to generate an unusual amount of benefit by solving a single problem.

33. B: Stable. If all of the data points on an *Np* chart fall between the upper and lower control limits, the process is stable. So long as all of the variation is within these limits, it can be assumed to be the result of common causes. Assuming the chart is reliable, data points that fall outside the upper and lower control limits are the result of special-cause variation. At the least, the presence of data points outside the upper and lower control limits identifies areas where employees will need to conduct further research. *Np* charts are control charts for analyzing attributes data. These charts are used when the sample size is regular and the targeted condition may only occur once per sample.

34. A: Process lead time. According to Little's law, the number of items included in a process divided by the number of process completions per hour is the process lead

time. Process cycle efficiency is calculated by dividing value-added time by process lead time. When every activity in the process adds value, the process may attain the maximum process cycle efficiency of 100%. Of course, very few processes actually reach this level of efficiency. It is much more common for a process to have a process cycle efficiency below 50%.

35. D: b. In nominal group technique, each participant should receive eight pieces of paper if there are 40 options to be considered. Each participant will then write one of the options down on each piece of paper, along with its rank (first through eighth). It is typical for each participant to receive eight pieces of paper when there are more than 35 options. When there are from 20 to 35 options, the typical number of papers for each person is six. When there are fewer than 20 options to be considered, it is typical for each member of the group to receive four pieces of paper. Once all of the group members turn in their rankings, the various options are compared, and the most popular are given further consideration.

36. A: P_p. When a batch sample has upper and lower specifications, the P_p statistic is used in the creation of a process performance index. If the batch sample has either an upper or a lower specification but not both, the P_{pk} statistic may be used. If the distributions are not normal, the C_p statistic is used to calculate the process performance indices.

37. C: Expense. Expense is not one of the factors included in the calculation of risk priority number. Risk priority number is calculated by multiplying severity, likelihood, and detection level. The severity of the risk is the significance of its occurrence. Various industries have created standardized tables for indicating the severity of common risks. The likelihood of a risk is simply the chances of it happening. Finally, the detection level is based on the number of modes for identifying the error or failure, as well as the chances that any one of these modes will be successful in detection. A common formula for calculating risk priority number is to place all of these categories on a scale from 1 to 10, then multiply them together. In this scenario, the maximum risk priority number would be 1,000.

38. B: Run test 6. Run test 6 identifies shifts in the process mean. The other run tests provide information about sampling errors. Run tests 1, 2, 3, and 5 also identify shifts in the process mean. Run tests are typically used in statistical process control programs to identify errors in data collection. Unfortunately, run tests are only able to identify the *presence* of errors and are not very good at pinpointing their location.

39. C: 0.9. An autocorrelation function of 0.9 would indicate the strongest correlation. The range of autocorrelation functions and partial autocorrelation functions extends from -1 to 1. The strength of the correlation is indicated by the distance from zero (that is, the absolute value), regardless of whether the value is on the positive or negative side. Therefore, an autocorrelation function of 0.9 would indicate a stronger correlation than would functions of 0.1, -0.8, and -0.2.

40. D: Poisson. A Poisson distribution should be used when the targeted characteristic may appear more than once per unit. In order for a Poisson distribution to be effective, the data should consist of positive whole numbers and the experimental trials should be independent. A binomial distribution is appropriate for situations in which the units in the population will only have one of two possible characteristics (for example, off or on). An exponential distribution is appropriate for measurement data, especially frequency. A lognormal distribution is appropriate for continuous data with a fixed lower boundary but no upper boundary. In most cases, the lower boundary of a lognormal distribution is zero.

41. C: DMAIC. The Six Sigma methodology of DMAIC (define, measure, analyze, improve, and control) is most appropriate for handling existing processes. It is geared toward gradual improvement. DMADV (define, measure, analyze, design, and verify), on the other hand, includes a design phase, during which new products can be developed. On occasion, DMADV is used to give existing products a large-scale remodeling. IDOV (identification, design, optimization, and validation) is the primary methodology of DFSS (design for Six Sigma). The main difference between DFSS and DMAIC is that the former attempts to prevent rather than reduce defects.

42. B: Poisson. A Poisson distribution would be most appropriate for discrete data. Binomial distributions may also be used for discrete data. Continuous data, on the other hand, should be handled with a normal, exponential, Johnson, or Pearson distribution. Continuous data is obtained from measurement, while discrete data is based on observation. A discrete data set, for instance, would only indicate the number of times an event occurred, but would not give any indication of the size or intensity of the event.

43. B: Kolmogorov-Smirnov test. The Kolmogorov-Smirnov test focuses on the relationship between number of data points and distributional fit. A nonparametric test is used instead of a hypothesis test for comparing the means from samples with different conditions and for assessing the effects of changes on process averages. A chi-square test is the simplest form of goodness-of-fit test. An Anderson-Darling test is excellent for obtaining information from the extreme ends of a distribution.

44. B: It is then easier to make adjustments later in the experiment. In hypothesis testing, it's better to set a *p* value than to select a significance level because it is then easier to make adjustments later in the experiment. In general, a *p* value allows for more freedom in the later parts of the experiment. There is always a possibility of rejecting a true hypothesis, in what is known as a Type 1 error. The number of samples collected is not dependent on whether a *p* value is set or a significance level is selected, and either method maintains the possibility that the null hypothesis will be rejected.

45. D: Diamonds. In the ANSI (American National Standards Institute) set of flowchart symbols, decisions are represented with diamonds. There are other symbols to represent different types of tasks, but many simple flowcharts will

simply use the diamond for decisions and rectangles for all other tasks in the process. An excessive number of decisions on a flowchart is a common symptom of inefficiency.

46. D: Improve. The 5S method is used most often during the improve stage of DMAIC. 5S is a Japanese lean tool for reducing cycle time. In Japanese, the five aspects of 5S are organization, purity, cleanliness, discipline, and tidiness. In English, these words are often translated as sort, straighten, shine, standardize, and sustain. The most common targets of 5S programs are processes that tend to lose materials or require unnecessary movement.

47. A: The square root of the total number of data values. In a histogram, the number of bars is equal to the square root of the total number of data values. Histograms look like bar graphs, but the bars on a histogram represent the number of observations that fall within a particular range. Histograms are often used to locate multiple distributions or apply a distribution to capability analysis. The width of each bar in a histogram is calculated by dividing the range of data by the number of bars. The range of data is determined by subtracting the minimum data value from the maximum data value. On a histogram, the x-axis represents the data values of each bar, and the y-axis indicates the number of observations.

48. D: Normal. A normal distribution is appropriate for continuous data with neither an upper nor a lower boundary. Continuous data is obtained through measurement. A lognormal or Weibull distribution is appropriate for sets of continuous data with a fixed lower boundary but no upper boundary. In most lognormal and Weibull distributions, the lower boundary is zero. An exponential distribution is appropriate for continuous data sets in which the values are relatively consistent.

49. A: First-order main effects. In a contour plot, a series of evenly spaced parallel lines indicates first-order main effects. Interactions between responses are indicated by curving contour lines. Very few contour plots consist of evenly spaced parallel lines. The most general use of contour plots is during the improve stage of DMAIC, when they are used in response surface analysis to predict minimum and maximum response values for specific data ranges.

50. C: A known standard deviation. A known standard deviation increases the power of an estimation of the confidence interval on the mean. Indeed, when the standard deviation is known, the z tables may be used to find the confidence interval on the mean; when the standard deviation is unknown, the t tables must be used. The confidence interval on the mean is the percentage of samples that will contain the true population mean. It is assumed that the sample population will follow a normal distribution. When there are more samples, this increases the power of the estimation of the confidence interval on the mean.

Secret Key #1 - Time is Your Greatest Enemy

Pace Yourself

Wear a watch. At the beginning of the test, check the time (or start a chronometer on your watch to count the minutes), and check the time after every few questions to make sure you are "on schedule."

If you are forced to speed up, do it efficiently. Usually one or more answer choices can be eliminated without too much difficulty. Above all, don't panic. Don't speed up and just begin guessing at random choices. By pacing yourself, and continually monitoring your progress against your watch, you will always know exactly how far ahead or behind you are with your available time. If you find that you are one minute behind on the test, don't skip one question without spending any time on it, just to catch back up. Take 15 fewer seconds on the next four questions, and after four questions you'll have caught back up. Once you catch back up, you can continue working each problem at your normal pace.

Furthermore, don't dwell on the problems that you were rushed on. If a problem was taking up too much time and you made a hurried guess, it must be difficult. The difficult questions are the ones you are most likely to miss anyway, so it isn't a big loss. It is better to end with more time than you need than to run out of time.

Lastly, sometimes it is beneficial to slow down if you are constantly getting ahead of time. You are always more likely to catch a careless mistake by working more slowly than quickly, and among very high-scoring test takers (those who are likely to have lots of time left over), careless errors affect the score more than mastery of material.

Secret Key #2 - Guessing is not Guesswork

You probably know that guessing is a good idea. Unlike other standardized tests, there is no penalty for getting a wrong answer. Even if you have no idea about a question, you still have a 20-25% chance of getting it right.

Most test takers do not understand the impact that proper guessing can have on their score. Unless you score extremely high, guessing will significantly contribute to your final score.

Monkeys Take the Test

What most test takers don't realize is that to insure that 20-25% chance, you have to guess randomly. If you put 20 monkeys in a room to take this test, assuming they answered once per question and behaved themselves, on average they would get 20-25% of the questions correct. Put 20 test takers in the room, and the average will be much lower among guessed questions. Why?
  1. The test writers intentionally write deceptive answer choices that "look" right. A test taker has no idea about a question, so he picks the "best looking" answer, which is often wrong. The monkey has no idea what looks good and what doesn't, so it will consistently be right about 20-25% of the time.
  2. Test takers will eliminate answer choices from the guessing pool based on a hunch or intuition. Simple but correct answers often get excluded, leaving a 0% chance of being correct. The monkey has no clue, and often gets lucky with the best choice.

This is why the process of elimination endorsed by most test courses is flawed and detrimental to your performance. Test takers don't guess; they make an ignorant stab in the dark that is usually worse than random.

$5 Challenge

Let me introduce one of the most valuable ideas of this course—the $5 challenge:

You only mark your "best guess" if you are willing to bet $5 on it.
You only eliminate choices from guessing if you are willing to bet $5 on it.

Why $5? Five dollars is an amount of money that is small yet not insignificant, and can really add up fast (20 questions could cost you $100). Likewise, each answer choice on one question of the test will have a small impact on your overall score, but it can really add up to a lot of points in the end.

The process of elimination IS valuable. The following shows your chance of guessing it right:

If you eliminate wrong answer choices until only this many remain:	Chance of getting it correct:
1	100%
2	50%
3	33%

However, if you accidentally eliminate the right answer or go on a hunch for an incorrect answer, your chances drop dramatically—to 0%. By guessing among all the answer choices, you are GUARANTEED to have a shot at the right answer.

That's why the $5 test is so valuable. If you give up the advantage and safety of a pure guess, it had better be worth the risk.

What we still haven't covered is how to be sure that whatever guess you make is truly random. Here's the easiest way:

Always pick the first answer choice among those remaining.

Such a technique means that you have decided, **before you see a single test question**, exactly how you are going to guess, and since the order of choices tells you nothing about which one is correct, this guessing technique is perfectly random.

This section is not meant to scare you away from making educated guesses or eliminating choices; you just need to define when a choice is worth eliminating. The $5 test, along with a pre-defined random guessing strategy, is the best way to make sure you reap all of the benefits of guessing.

Secret Key #3 - Practice Smarter, Not Harder

Many test takers delay the test preparation process because they dread the awful amounts of practice time they think necessary to succeed on the test. We have refined an effective method that will take you only a fraction of the time.

There are a number of "obstacles" in the path to success. Among these are answering questions, finishing in time, and mastering test-taking strategies. All must be executed on the day of the test at peak performance, or your score will suffer. The test is a mental marathon that has a large impact on your future.

Just like a marathon runner, it is important to work your way up to the full challenge. So first you just worry about questions, and then time, and finally strategy:

Success Strategy

1. Find a good source for practice tests.
2. If you are willing to make a larger time investment, consider using more than one study guide. Often the different approaches of multiple authors will help you "get" difficult concepts.
3. Take a practice test with no time constraints, with all study helps, "open book." Take your time with questions and focus on applying strategies.
4. Take a practice test with time constraints, with all guides, "open book."
5. Take a final practice test without open material and with time limits.

If you have time to take more practice tests, just repeat step 5. By gradually exposing yourself to the full rigors of the test environment, you will condition your mind to the stress of test day and maximize your success.

Secret Key #4 - Prepare, Don't Procrastinate

Let me state an obvious fact: if you take the test three times, you will probably get three different scores. This is due to the way you feel on test day, the level of preparedness you have, and the version of the test you see. Despite the test writers' claims to the contrary, some versions of the test WILL be easier for you than others.

Since your future depends so much on your score, you should maximize your chances of success. In order to maximize the likelihood of success, you've got to prepare in advance. This means taking practice tests and spending time learning the information and test taking strategies you will need to succeed.

Never go take the actual test as a "practice" test, expecting that you can just take it again if you need to. Take all the practice tests you can on your own, but when you go to take the official test, be prepared, be focused, and do your best the first time!

Secret Key #5 - Test Yourself

Everyone knows that time is money. There is no need to spend too much of your time or too little of your time preparing for the test. You should only spend as much of your precious time preparing as is necessary for you to get the score you need.

Once you have taken a practice test under real conditions of time constraints, then you will know if you are ready for the test or not.

If you have scored extremely high the first time that you take the practice test, then there is not much point in spending countless hours studying. You are already there.

Benchmark your abilities by retaking practice tests and seeing how much you have improved. Once you consistently score high enough to guarantee success, then you are ready.

If you have scored well below where you need, then knuckle down and begin studying in earnest. Check your improvement regularly through the use of practice tests under real conditions. Above all, don't worry, panic, or give up. The key is perseverance!

Then, when you go to take the test, remain confident and remember how well you did on the practice tests. If you can score high enough on a practice test, then you can do the same on the real thing.

General Strategies

The most important thing you can do is to ignore your fears and jump into the test immediately. Do not be overwhelmed by any strange-sounding terms. You have to jump into the test like jumping into a pool—all at once is the easiest way.

Make Predictions

As you read and understand the question, try to guess what the answer will be. Remember that several of the answer choices are wrong, and once you begin reading them, your mind will immediately become cluttered with answer choices designed to throw you off. Your mind is typically the most focused immediately after you have read the question and digested its contents. If you can, try to predict what the correct answer will be. You may be surprised at what you can predict.

Quickly scan the choices and see if your prediction is in the listed answer choices. If it is, then you can be quite confident that you have the right answer. It still won't hurt to check the other answer choices, but most of the time, you've got it!

Answer the Question

It may seem obvious to only pick answer choices that answer the question, but the test writers can create some excellent answer choices that are wrong. Don't pick an answer just because it sounds right, or you believe it to be true. It MUST answer the question. Once you've made your selection, always go back and check it against the question and make sure that you didn't misread the question and that the answer choice does answer the question posed.

Benchmark

After you read the first answer choice, decide if you think it sounds correct or not. If it doesn't, move on to the next answer choice. If it does, mentally mark that answer choice. This doesn't mean that you've definitely selected it as your answer choice, it just means that it's the best you've seen thus far. Go ahead and read the next choice. If the next choice is worse than the one you've already selected, keep going to the next answer choice. If the next choice is better than the choice you've already selected, mentally mark the new answer choice as your best guess.

The first answer choice that you select becomes your standard. Every other answer choice must be benchmarked against that standard. That choice is correct until proven otherwise by another answer choice beating it out. Once you've decided that no other answer choice seems as good, do one final check to ensure that your answer choice answers the question posed.

Valid Information

Don't discount any of the information provided in the question. Every piece of information may be necessary to determine the correct answer. None of the information in the question is there to throw you off (while the answer choices will certainly have information to throw you off). If two seemingly unrelated topics are discussed, don't ignore either. You can be confident there is a relationship, or it wouldn't be included in the question, and you are probably going to have to determine what is that relationship to find the answer.

Avoid "Fact Traps"

Don't get distracted by a choice that is factually true. Your search is for the answer that answers the question. Stay focused and don't fall for an answer that is true but irrelevant. Always go back to the question and make sure you're choosing an answer that actually answers the question and is not just a true statement. An answer can be factually correct, but it MUST answer the question asked. Additionally, two answers can both be seemingly correct, so be sure to read all of the answer choices, and make sure that you get the one that BEST answers the question.

Milk the Question

Some of the questions may throw you completely off. They might deal with a subject you have not been exposed to, or one that you haven't reviewed in years. While your lack of knowledge about the subject will be a hindrance, the question itself can give you many clues that will help you find the correct answer. Read the question carefully and look for clues. Watch particularly for adjectives and nouns describing difficult terms or words that you don't recognize. Regardless of whether you completely understand a word or not, replacing it with a synonym, either provided or one you more familiar with, may help you to understand what the questions are asking. Rather than wracking your mind about specific detailed information concerning a difficult term or word, try to use mental substitutes that are easier to understand.

The Trap of Familiarity

Don't just choose a word because you recognize it. On difficult questions, you may not recognize a number of words in the answer choices. The test writers don't put "make-believe" words on the test, so don't think that just because you only recognize all the words in one answer choice that that answer choice must be correct. If you only recognize words in one answer choice, then focus on that one. Is it correct? Try your best to determine if it is correct. If it is, that's great. If not, eliminate it. Each word and answer choice you eliminate increases your chances of getting the question correct, even if you then have to guess among the unfamiliar choices.

Eliminate Answers

Eliminate choices as soon as you realize they are wrong. But be careful! Make sure you consider all of the possible answer choices. Just because one appears right, doesn't mean that the next one won't be even better! The test writers will usually put more than one good answer choice for every question, so read all of them. Don't worry if you are stuck between two that seem right. By getting down to just two remaining possible choices, your odds are now 50/50. Rather than wasting too much time, play the odds. You are guessing, but guessing wisely because you've been able to knock out some of the answer choices that you know are wrong. If you are eliminating choices and realize that the last answer choice you are left with is also obviously wrong, don't panic. Start over and consider each choice again. There may easily be something that you missed the first time and will realize on the second pass.

Tough Questions

If you are stumped on a problem or it appears too hard or too difficult, don't waste time. Move on! Remember though, if you can quickly check for obviously incorrect answer choices, your chances of guessing correctly are greatly improved. Before you completely give up, at least try to knock out a couple of possible answers. Eliminate what you can and then guess at the remaining answer choices before moving on.

Brainstorm

If you get stuck on a difficult question, spend a few seconds quickly brainstorming. Run through the complete list of possible answer choices. Look at each choice and ask yourself, "Could this answer the question satisfactorily?" Go through each answer choice and consider it independently of the others. By systematically going through all possibilities, you may find something that you would otherwise overlook. Remember though that when you get stuck, it's important to try to keep moving.

Read Carefully

Understand the problem. Read the question and answer choices carefully. Don't miss the question because you misread the terms. You have plenty of time to read each question thoroughly and make sure you understand what is being asked. Yet a happy medium must be attained, so don't waste too much time. You must read carefully, but efficiently.

Face Value

When in doubt, use common sense. Always accept the situation in the problem at face value. Don't read too much into it. These problems will not require you to make huge leaps of logic. The test writers aren't trying to throw you off with a cheap trick. If you have to go beyond creativity and make a leap of logic in order to have an answer choice answer the question, then you should look at the other answer choices. Don't overcomplicate the problem by creating theoretical relationships or explanations that will warp time or space. These are normal problems rooted in reality. It's just that the applicable relationship or explanation may not be readily apparent and you have to figure things out. Use your common sense to interpret anything that isn't clear.

Prefixes

If you're having trouble with a word in the question or answer choices, try dissecting it. Take advantage of every clue that the word might include. Prefixes and suffixes can be a huge help. Usually they allow you to determine a basic meaning. Pre- means before, post- means after, pro - is positive, de- is negative. From these prefixes and suffixes, you can get an idea of the general meaning of the word and try to put it into context. Beware though of any traps. Just because con- is the opposite of pro-, doesn't necessarily mean congress is the opposite of progress!

Hedge Phrases

Watch out for critical hedge phrases, led off with words such as "likely," "may," "can," "sometimes," "often," "almost," "mostly," "usually," "generally," "rarely," and "sometimes." Question writers insert these hedge phrases to cover every possibility. Often an answer choice will be wrong simply because it leaves no room for exception. Unless the situation calls for them, avoid answer choices that have definitive words like "exactly," and "always."

Switchback Words

Stay alert for "switchbacks." These are the words and phrases frequently used to alert you to shifts in thought. The most common switchback word is "but." Others include "although," "however," "nevertheless," "on the other hand," "even though," "while," "in spite of," "despite," and "regardless of."

New Information

Correct answer choices will rarely have completely new information included. Answer choices typically are straightforward reflections of the material asked about and will directly relate to the question. If a new piece of information is included in an answer choice that doesn't even seem to relate to the topic being asked about, then that answer choice is likely incorrect. All of the information needed to answer the question is usually provided for you in the question. You should not have to make guesses that are unsupported or choose answer choices that require unknown information that cannot be reasoned from what is given.

Time Management

On technical questions, don't get lost on the technical terms. Don't spend too much time on any one question. If you don't know what a term means, then odds are you aren't going to get much further since you don't have a dictionary. You should be able to immediately recognize whether or not you know a term. If you don't, work with the other clues that you have—the other answer choices and terms provided— but don't waste too much time trying to figure out a difficult term that you don't know.

Contextual Clues

Look for contextual clues. An answer can be right but not the correct answer. The contextual clues will help you find the answer that is most right and is correct. Understand the context in which a phrase or statement is made. This will help you make important distinctions.

Don't Panic

Panicking will not answer any questions for you; therefore, it isn't helpful. When you first see the question, if your mind goes blank, take a deep breath. Force yourself to mechanically go through the steps of solving the problem using the strategies you've learned.

Pace Yourself

Don't get clock fever. It's easy to be overwhelmed when you're looking at a page full of questions, your mind is full of random thoughts and feeling confused, and the clock is ticking down faster than you would like. Calm down and maintain the pace that you have set for yourself. As long as you are on track by monitoring your pace, you are guaranteed to have enough time for yourself. When you get to the last few minutes of the test, it may seem like you won't have enough time left, but if you only have as many questions as you should have left at that point, then you're right on track!

Answer Selection

The best way to pick an answer choice is to eliminate all of those that are wrong, until only one is left and confirm that is the correct answer. Sometimes though, an answer choice may immediately look right. Be careful! Take a second to make sure that the other choices are not equally obvious. Don't make a hasty mistake. There are only two times that you should stop before checking other answers. First is when you are positive that the answer choice you have selected is correct. Second is when time is almost out and you have to make a quick guess!

Check Your Work

Since you will probably not know every term listed and the answer to every question, it is important that you get credit for the ones that you do know. Don't miss any questions through careless mistakes. If at all possible, try to take a second to look back over your answer selection and make sure you've selected the correct answer choice and haven't made a costly careless mistake (such as marking an answer choice that you didn't mean to mark). The time it takes for this quick double check should more than pay for itself in caught mistakes.

Beware of Directly Quoted Answers

Sometimes an answer choice will repeat word for word a portion of the question or reference section. However, beware of such exact duplication. It may be a trap! More than likely, the correct choice will paraphrase or summarize a point, rather than being exactly the same wording.

Slang

Scientific sounding answers are better than slang ones. An answer choice that begins "To compare the outcomes…" is much more likely to be correct than one that begins "Because some people insisted…"

Extreme Statements

Avoid wild answers that throw out highly controversial ideas that are proclaimed as established fact. An answer choice that states the "process should used in certain situations, if..." is much more likely to be correct than one that states the "process should be discontinued completely." The first is a calm rational statement and doesn't even make a definitive, uncompromising stance, using a hedge word "if" to provide wiggle room, whereas the second choice is a radical idea and far more extreme.

Answer Choice Families

When you have two or more answer choices that are direct opposites or parallels, one of them is usually the correct answer. For instance, if one answer choice states "x increases" and another answer choice states "x decreases" or "y increases," then those two or three answer choices are very similar in construction and fall into the same family of answer choices. A family of answer choices consists of two or three answer choices, very similar in construction, but often with directly opposite meanings. Usually the correct answer choice will be in that family of answer choices. The "odd man out" or answer choice that doesn't seem to fit the parallel construction of the other answer choices is more likely to be incorrect.

Special Report: How to Overcome Test Anxiety

The very nature of tests caters to some level of anxiety, nervousness, or tension, just as we feel for any important event that occurs in our lives. A little bit of anxiety or nervousness can be a good thing. It helps us with motivation, and makes achievement just that much sweeter. However, too much anxiety can be a problem, especially if it hinders our ability to function and perform.

"Test anxiety," is the term that refers to the emotional reactions that some test-takers experience when faced with a test or exam. Having a fear of testing and exams is based upon a rational fear, since the test-taker's performance can shape the course of an academic career. Nevertheless, experiencing excessive fear of examinations will only interfere with the test-taker's ability to perform and chance to be successful.

There are a large variety of causes that can contribute to the development and sensation of test anxiety. These include, but are not limited to, lack of preparation and worrying about issues surrounding the test.

Lack of Preparation

Lack of preparation can be identified by the following behaviors or situations:

Not scheduling enough time to study, and therefore cramming the night before the test or exam
Managing time poorly, to create the sensation that there is not enough time to do everything
Failing to organize the text information in advance, so that the study material consists of the entire text and not simply the pertinent information
Poor overall studying habits

Worrying, on the other hand, can be related to both the test taker, or many other factors around him/her that will be affected by the results of the test. These include worrying about:

Previous performances on similar exams, or exams in general
How friends and other students are achieving
The negative consequences that will result from a poor grade or failure

There are three primary elements to test anxiety. Physical components, which involve the same typical bodily reactions as those to acute anxiety (to be discussed below). Emotional factors have to do with fear or panic. Mental or cognitive issues concerning attention spans and memory abilities.

Physical Signals

There are many different symptoms of test anxiety, and these are not limited to mental and emotional strain. Frequently there are a range of physical signals that will let a test taker know that he/she is suffering from test anxiety. These bodily changes can include the following:

Perspiring
Sweaty palms
Wet, trembling hands
Nausea
Dry mouth
A knot in the stomach
Headache
Faintness
Muscle tension
Aching shoulders, back and neck
Rapid heart beat
Feeling too hot/cold

To recognize the sensation of test anxiety, a test-taker should monitor him/herself for the following sensations:

The physical distress symptoms as listed above
Emotional sensitivity, expressing emotional feelings such as the need to cry or laugh too much, or a sensation of anger or helplessness
A decreased ability to think, causing the test-taker to blank out or have racing thoughts that are hard to organize or control.

Though most students will feel some level of anxiety when faced with a test or exam, the majority can cope with that anxiety and maintain it at a manageable level. However, those who cannot are faced with a very real and very serious condition, which can and should be controlled for the immeasurable benefit of this sufferer.

Naturally, these sensations lead to negative results for the testing experience. The most common effects of test anxiety have to do with nervousness and mental blocking.

Nervousness

Nervousness can appear in several different levels:

The test-taker's difficulty, or even inability to read and understand the questions on the test

The difficulty or inability to organize thoughts to a coherent form
The difficulty or inability to recall key words and concepts relating to the testing questions (especially essays)
The receipt of poor grades on a test, though the test material was well known by the test taker

Conversely, a person may also experience mental blocking, which involves:

Blanking out on test questions
Only remembering the correct answers to the questions when the test has already finished.

Fortunately for test anxiety sufferers, beating these feelings, to a large degree, has to do with proper preparation. When a test taker has a feeling of preparedness, then anxiety will be dramatically lessened.

The first step to resolving anxiety issues is to distinguish which of the two types of anxiety are being suffered. If the anxiety is a direct result of a lack of preparation, this should be considered a normal reaction, and the anxiety level (as opposed to the test results) shouldn't be anything to worry about. However, if, when adequately prepared, the test-taker still panics, blanks out, or seems to overreact, this is not a fully rational reaction. While this can be considered normal too, there are many ways to combat and overcome these effects.

Remember that anxiety cannot be entirely eliminated, however, there are ways to minimize it, to make the anxiety easier to manage. Preparation is one of the best ways to minimize test anxiety. Therefore the following techniques are wise in order to best fight off any anxiety that may want to build.

To begin with, try to avoid cramming before a test, whenever it is possible. By trying to memorize an entire term's worth of information in one day, you'll be shocking your system, and not giving yourself a very good chance to absorb the information. This is an easy path to anxiety, so for those who suffer from test anxiety, cramming should not even be considered an option.

Instead of cramming, work throughout the semester to combine all of the material which is presented throughout the semester, and work on it gradually as the course goes by, making sure to master the main concepts first, leaving minor details for a week or so before the test.

To study for the upcoming exam, be sure to pose questions that may be on the examination, to gauge the ability to answer them by integrating the ideas from your texts, notes and lectures, as well as any supplementary readings.

If it is truly impossible to cover all of the information that was covered in that particular term, concentrate on the most important portions, that can be covered very well. Learn these concepts as best as possible, so that when the test comes, a goal can be made to use these concepts as presentations of your knowledge.

In addition to study habits, changes in attitude are critical to beating a struggle with test anxiety. In fact, an improvement of the perspective over the entire test-taking experience can actually help a test taker to enjoy studying and therefore improve the overall experience. Be certain not to overemphasize the significance of the grade - know that the result of the test is neither a reflection of self worth, nor is it a measure of intelligence; one grade will not predict a person's future success.

To improve an overall testing outlook, the following steps should be tried:

Keeping in mind that the most reasonable expectation for taking a test is to expect to try to demonstrate as much of what you know as you possibly can. Reminding ourselves that a test is only one test; this is not the only one, and there will be others.
The thought of thinking of oneself in an irrational, all-or-nothing term should be avoided at all costs.
A reward should be designated for after the test, so there's something to look forward to. Whether it be going to a movie, going out to eat, or simply visiting friends, schedule it in advance, and do it no matter what result is expected on the exam.

Test-takers should also keep in mind that the basics are some of the most important things, even beyond anti-anxiety techniques and studying. Never neglect the basic social, emotional and biological needs, in order to try to absorb information. In order to best achieve, these three factors must be held as just as important as the studying itself.

Study Steps

Remember the following important steps for studying:

Maintain healthy nutrition and exercise habits. Continue both your recreational activities and social pass times. These both contribute to your physical and emotional well being.
Be certain to get a good amount of sleep, especially the night before the test, because when you're overtired you are not able to perform to the best of your best ability.
Keep the studying pace to a moderate level by taking breaks when they are needed, and varying the work whenever possible, to keep the mind fresh instead of getting bored.
When enough studying has been done that all the material that can be learned has been learned, and the test taker is prepared for the test, stop studying and do

something relaxing such as listening to music, watching a movie, or taking a warm bubble bath.

There are also many other techniques to minimize the uneasiness or apprehension that is experienced along with test anxiety before, during, or even after the examination. In fact, there are a great deal of things that can be done to stop anxiety from interfering with lifestyle and performance. Again, remember that anxiety will not be eliminated entirely, and it shouldn't be. Otherwise that "up" feeling for exams would not exist, and most of us depend on that sensation to perform better than usual. However, this anxiety has to be at a level that is manageable.

Of course, as we have just discussed, being prepared for the exam is half the battle right away. Attending all classes, finding out what knowledge will be expected on the exam, and knowing the exam schedules are easy steps to lowering anxiety. Keeping up with work will remove the need to cram, and efficient study habits will eliminate wasted time. Studying should be done in an ideal location for concentration, so that it is simple to become interested in the material and give it complete attention. A method such as SQ3R (Survey, Question, Read, Recite, Review) is a wonderful key to follow to make sure that the study habits are as effective as possible, especially in the case of learning from a textbook. Flashcards are great techniques for memorization. Learning to take good notes will mean that notes will be full of useful information, so that less sifting will need to be done to seek out what is pertinent for studying. Reviewing notes after class and then again on occasion will keep the information fresh in the mind. From notes that have been taken summary sheets and outlines can be made for simpler reviewing.

A study group can also be a very motivational and helpful place to study, as there will be a sharing of ideas, all of the minds can work together, to make sure that everyone understands, and the studying will be made more interesting because it will be a social occasion.

Basically, though, as long as the test-taker remains organized and self confident, with efficient study habits, less time will need to be spent studying, and higher grades will be achieved.

To become self confident, there are many useful steps. The first of these is "self talk." It has been shown through extensive research, that self-talk for students who suffer from test anxiety, should be well monitored, in order to make sure that it contributes to self confidence as opposed to sinking the student. Frequently the self talk of test-anxious students is negative or self-defeating, thinking that everyone else is smarter and faster, that they always mess up, and that if they don't do well, they'll fail the entire course. It is important to decreasing anxiety that awareness is made of self talk. Try writing any negative self thoughts and then disputing them with a positive statement instead. Begin

- 106 -

self-encouragement as though it was a friend speaking. Repeat positive statements to help reprogram the mind to believing in successes instead of failures.

Helpful Techniques

Other extremely helpful techniques include:

Self-visualization of doing well and reaching goals
While aiming for an "A" level of understanding, don't try to "overprotect" by setting your expectations lower. This will only convince the mind to stop studying in order to meet the lower expectations.
Don't make comparisons with the results or habits of other students. These are individual factors, and different things work for different people, causing different results.
Strive to become an expert in learning what works well, and what can be done in order to improve. Consider collecting this data in a journal.
Create rewards for after studying instead of doing things before studying that will only turn into avoidance behaviors.
Make a practice of relaxing - by using methods such as progressive relaxation, self-hypnosis, guided imagery, etc - in order to make relaxation an automatic sensation.
Work on creating a state of relaxed concentration so that concentrating will take on the focus of the mind, so that none will be wasted on worrying.
Take good care of the physical self by eating well and getting enough sleep.
Plan in time for exercise and stick to this plan.

Beyond these techniques, there are other methods to be used before, during and after the test that will help the test-taker perform well in addition to overcoming anxiety.

Before the exam comes the academic preparation. This involves establishing a study schedule and beginning at least one week before the actual date of the test. By doing this, the anxiety of not having enough time to study for the test will be automatically eliminated. Moreover, this will make the studying a much more effective experience, ensuring that the learning will be an easier process. This relieves much undue pressure on the test-taker.

Summary sheets, note cards, and flash cards with the main concepts and examples of these main concepts should be prepared in advance of the actual studying time. A topic should never be eliminated from this process. By omitting a topic because it isn't expected to be on the test is only setting up the test-taker for anxiety should it actually appear on the exam. Utilize the course syllabus for laying out the topics that should be studied. Carefully go over the notes that were made in class, paying special attention to any of the issues that the professor took special care to emphasize while lecturing in class. In the textbooks, use the chapter review, or if possible, the chapter tests, to begin your review.

It may even be possible to ask the instructor what information will be covered on the exam, or what the format of the exam will be (for example, multiple choice, essay, free form, true-false). Additionally, see if it is possible to find out how many questions will be on the test. If a review sheet or sample test has been offered by the professor, make good use of it, above anything else, for the preparation for the test. Another great resource for getting to know the examination is reviewing tests from previous semesters. Use these tests to review, and aim to achieve a 100% score on each of the possible topics. With a few exceptions, the goal that you set for yourself is the highest one that you will reach.

Take all of the questions that were assigned as homework, and rework them to any other possible course material. The more problems reworked, the more skill and confidence will form as a result. When forming the solution to a problem, write out each of the steps. Don't simply do head work. By doing as many steps on paper as possible, much clarification and therefore confidence will be formed. Do this with as many homework problems as possible, before checking the answers. By checking the answer after each problem, a reinforcement will exist, that will not be on the exam. Study situations should be as exam-like as possible, to prime the test-taker's system for the experience. By waiting to check the answers at the end, a psychological advantage will be formed, to decrease the stress factor.

Another fantastic reason for not cramming is the avoidance of confusion in concepts, especially when it comes to mathematics. 8-10 hours of study will become one hundred percent more effective if it is spread out over a week or at least several days, instead of doing it all in one sitting. Recognize that the human brain requires time in order to assimilate new material, so frequent breaks and a span of study time over several days will be much more beneficial.

Additionally, don't study right up until the point of the exam. Studying should stop a minimum of one hour before the exam begins. This allows the brain to rest and put things in their proper order. This will also provide the time to become as relaxed as possible when going into the examination room. The test-taker will also have time to eat well and eat sensibly. Know that the brain needs food as much as the rest of the body. With enough food and enough sleep, as well as a relaxed attitude, the body and the mind are primed for success.

Avoid any anxious classmates who are talking about the exam. These students only spread anxiety, and are not worth sharing the anxious sentimentalities.

Before the test also involves creating a positive attitude, so mental preparation should also be a point of concentration. There are many keys to creating a positive attitude. Should fears become rushing in, make a visualization of taking the exam, doing well, and seeing an A written on the paper. Write out a list of affirmations that will bring a feeling of confidence, such as "I am doing well in my English class," "I studied well and know my material," "I enjoy this class." Even if the affirmations aren't believed at first, it sends a positive message to the subconscious which will result in an alteration of the overall belief system, which is the system that creates reality.

If a sensation of panic begins, work with the fear and imagine the very worst! Work through the entire scenario of not passing the test, failing the entire course, and dropping out of school, followed by not getting a job, and pushing a shopping cart through the dark alley where you'll live. This will place things into perspective! Then, practice deep breathing and create a visualization of the opposite situation - achieving an "A" on the exam, passing the entire course, receiving the degree at a graduation ceremony.

On the day of the test, there are many things to be done to ensure the best results, as well as the most calm outlook. The following stages are suggested in order to maximize test-taking potential:

Begin the examination day with a moderate breakfast, and avoid any coffee or beverages with caffeine if the test taker is prone to jitters. Even people who are used to managing caffeine can feel jittery or light-headed when it is taken on a test day.
Attempt to do something that is relaxing before the examination begins. As last minute cramming clouds the mastering of overall concepts, it is better to use this time to create a calming outlook.
Be certain to arrive at the test location well in advance, in order to provide time to select a location that is away from doors, windows and other distractions, as well as giving enough time to relax before the test begins.
Keep away from anxiety generating classmates who will upset the sensation of stability and relaxation that is being attempted before the exam.
Should the waiting period before the exam begins cause anxiety, create a self-distraction by reading a light magazine or something else that is relaxing and simple.

During the exam itself, read the entire exam from beginning to end, and find out how much time should be allotted to each individual problem. Once writing the exam, should more time be taken for a problem, it should be abandoned, in order to begin another problem. If there is time at the end, the unfinished problem can always be returned to and completed.

Read the instructions very carefully - twice - so that unpleasant surprises won't follow during or after the exam has ended.

When writing the exam, pretend that the situation is actually simply the completion of homework within a library, or at home. This will assist in forming a relaxed atmosphere, and will allow the brain extra focus for the complex thinking function.

Begin the exam with all of the questions with which the most confidence is felt. This will build the confidence level regarding the entire exam and will begin a quality momentum. This will also create encouragement for trying the problems where uncertainty resides.

Going with the "gut instinct" is always the way to go when solving a problem. Second guessing should be avoided at all costs. Have confidence in the ability to do well.

For essay questions, create an outline in advance that will keep the mind organized and make certain that all of the points are remembered. For multiple choice, read every answer, even if the correct one has been spotted - a better one may exist.

Continue at a pace that is reasonable and not rushed, in order to be able to work carefully. Provide enough time to go over the answers at the end, to check for small errors that can be corrected.

Should a feeling of panic begin, breathe deeply, and think of the feeling of the body releasing sand through its pores. Visualize a calm, peaceful place, and include all of the sights, sounds and sensations of this image. Continue the deep breathing, and take a few minutes to continue this with closed eyes. When all is well again, return to the test.

If a "blanking" occurs for a certain question, skip it and move on to the next question. There will be time to return to the other question later. Get everything done that can be done, first, to guarantee all the grades that can be compiled, and to build all of the confidence possible. Then return to the weaker questions to build the marks from there.

Remember, one's own reality can be created, so as long as the belief is there, success will follow. And remember: anxiety can happen later, right now, there's an exam to be written!

After the examination is complete, whether there is a feeling for a good grade or a bad grade, don't dwell on the exam, and be certain to follow through on the reward that was promised...and enjoy it! Don't dwell on any mistakes that have been made, as there is nothing that can be done at this point anyway.

Additionally, don't begin to study for the next test right away. Do something relaxing for a while, and let the mind relax and prepare itself to begin absorbing information again.

From the results of the exam - both the grade and the entire experience, be certain to learn from what has gone on. Perfect studying habits and work some more on confidence in order to make the next examination experience even better than the last one.

Learn to avoid places where openings occurred for laziness, procrastination and day dreaming.

Use the time between this exam and the next one to better learn to relax, even learning to relax on cue, so that any anxiety can be controlled during the next exam. Learn how to relax the body. Slouch in your chair if that helps. Tighten and then relax all of the different muscle groups, one group at a time, beginning with the feet and then working all the way up to the neck and face. This will ultimately relax the muscles more than they were to begin with. Learn how to breathe deeply and comfortably, and focus on this breathing going in and out as a relaxing thought. With every exhale, repeat the word "relax."

As common as test anxiety is, it is very possible to overcome it. Make yourself one of the test-takers who overcome this frustrating hindrance.

Additional Bonus Material

Due to our efforts to try to keep this book to a manageable length, we've created a link that will give you access to all of your additional bonus material.

Please visit http://www.mometrix.com/bonus948/sixsigmagb to access the information.